W

TRAINING
WITH A BEAT

TRAINING
WITH A BEAT

The Teaching Power of Music

Lenn Millbower

Foreword by Margaret Parkin

Stylus
PUBLISHING, LLC.

Sterling, Virginia

Copyright © 2000 by Stylus Publishing, LLC

Published by Stylus Publishing, LLC
22841 Quicksilver Drive
Sterling, Virginia 20166-2012

Stylus is a registered trademark of Stylus Publishing, LLC

Library of Congress Cataloging-in-Publication Data

Millbower, Lenn, 1951–
  Training with a beat : the teaching power of music / Lenn Millbower ; with illustrations.— 1st ed.
      p.   cm.
  Includes bibliographical references (p.) and index.
  ISBN 1-57922-000-2
    1. Music—Psychological aspects. 2. Music, Influence of. 3. Music in education.   I. Title.

ML3830 .M73 2000
781'.071—dc21

                                                                00-022195

Printed in Canada on acid-free paper that meets the American National Standards Institute Z39-48 Standard.

Designed by Pen & Palette Unlimited

First Edition

10 9 8 7 6 5 4 3 2 1

To Roger Benedict—Your voice
is silent, but your music lives.

CONTENTS

FOREWORD

Reading Lenn Millbower's book for the first time reminded me of a family story that my mother used to take great delight in telling—usually at times of maximum embarrassment—of my apparent penchant as a small baby for sitting up in my pram, pointing a chubby finger at the large ugly radio on the kitchen table, and shouting "Moo-gick! Moo-gick!" inconsolably until someone took pity on me and turned the thing on. My mother obviously took this behavior to be the early signs of a young Rachmaninoff in the making. Sadly—and like so many other proud mothers of her day—she was wrong.

However, on a happier note, my love of "moo-gick" . . . I'm sorry, music . . . is something that has stayed with me over the years, and even now it would be difficult for me to imagine a world in which it did not feature prominently—both in my personal life and in my professional role as a trainer and speaker in management and personal development.

As trainers, whatever our field of education, the pressure is always on us—and increasingly so in this new millennium—to find better, more effective, and longer-lasting ways of getting our message across; and while twenty-first-century technology clearly plays its part in that endeavor, I often wonder whether it can touch the heart and stir the emotions in the same way music can. Personally, I doubt it.

Research carried out by the likes of Gardner and Losanov has already proved music to be a powerful teaching tool, which acknowledges and maximizes the brain's natural learning abilities. Lenn's book builds on those foundations and gives us practical tools and techniques that bring the theories to life—just in the same way that black dots on a manuscript can give birth to song.

Lenn's book is a pain-free, fun, and thought-provoking introduction that should overcome any hesitation you might have about using music in training. No need here to struggle—as I did as a student—over scales, arpeggios, and chromatics. I can guarantee it.

Lenn's question, "When was the last time people left your classroom singing?" is certainly one that is still ringing in *my* ears.

Margaret Parkin
January 2000

ACKNOWLEDGMENTS

A book of this magnitude would be impossible without the assistance and support of a large number of people. I would like to publicly thank them.

To the publisher, John von Knorring, for believing in this project.

To the professional colleagues who aided and furthered my career: Cindy Anderson, for sound professional advice; Rodney Miller, for shining a beacon to light my way; and to Jody Baldwin, Nancy Gidusko, Greg Wann, Teri Hamel, Stephen Hoel, Jim Martin, Sharon Madill, Rodney Miller, Mark Potter, John Spano, Judy Rosser, Penny Hightower, and all the others whom I neglected to mention.

To the teachers who helped me find my beat. Angela Rivers, whose words fated me to pursue music; Doris Yager, who started me on the path and provided continued support through many years of ups and downs; Philip Korn, who encouraged me to examine anything that caught my curiosity; and Ray Keppel, John Miller, and Ron Zollweg, who inspired a love of performing in me.

To the friends who always knew I could, and did not care if I could not: John Franklin, Steve Kane, Larry and Denise Lessard, Gary Marchetti, Michelle Pagan, and Stephen Superak.

To my brothers, sister, relatives, and father for being there; to my mother for believing; and to my wife, whose many hours of widowhood made this book possible.

Top Ten Reasons to Use Music in Learning

10. Music adds life to otherwise dull material.

9. Music taps into people's emotions.

8. Music honors the diversity of your learners.

7. People will want to attend your sessions.

6. Your learners will sing your "phrases."

5. Your Level One Evaluations will all be "5s with a beat."

4. Your coworkers will be impressed with your expertise.

3. You can play your favorite CDs at work.

2. Your CD collection will be tax deductible.

1. Your boss won't want to lose you or your beat during the next cutbacks.

PROLOGUE

Welcome to *Training with a Beat: The Teaching Power of Music*. This book started out as a curiosity. In my first career, I was a performing musician-magician, leading a troupe of performers that combined music and entertainment in new, unique ways. A typical night started with light musical material and ended with high-energy dance music. Along the way, the audience would experience a magical-musical extravaganza. The act's repertoire of unique presentations included burning our female vocalist alive to Michael Jackson's "Thriller" and floating her above the dance floor in time with the Beatles song "Lucy in the Sky with Diamonds." Through ten years of multiple incarnations, my performers and I traveled the North American continent, performing in prestigious and unpretentious surroundings, for all sorts of people, with vastly different needs and wildly varying circumstances.

Our act was noted for its responsiveness to the audience—a flexibility that resulted from the unusual way we decided, song to song, which piece of material, or illusion, to perform. We rarely followed a predetermined "set" order. Our dual responsibilities were to the venue owner and our patrons—making a profit for the owner while pleasing our audience. We met both needs by performing music that modified the audience's behavior. Through music, we would encourage people to dance, buy drinks, socialize, and dance again—repeating this cycle all night, so that the venue made money and people enjoyed themselves without overindulging.

Through years of audience observation, I noticed some repeating trends. Specific songs generated predictable audience responses. One selection would generate anxiety, the next excitement, or sadness, or friendliness, or romance, or pride. It was a revelation:

I could control the mood of the audience by simply selecting the right song!

By the time my instruments were packed and my magic put away, I had developed a broad understanding of music's relationship to individual and group dynamics.

My next careers took me back to college and teaching stints in both the corporate and college environments. Almost by instinct, I began applying my musical behavior modification techniques to adult-learning situations. After all, an effective teacher must gain the adult learner's attention, communicate information once that learner is prepared to learn, and help the learner hone his or her skills. As you will soon discover, music is a resource for achieving these ends. I present *Training with a Beat: The Teaching Power of Music* in the hope that it will help you and adult-learning instructors, facilitators, presenters, and teachers everywhere tap into this often-overlooked learning resource.

By reading *Training with a Beat: The Teaching Power of Music,* you will:

- discover interrelationships between learning theories and music

- comprehend basic music theory principles relevant to learning

- learn musical games and activities applicable to learning situations

- select music appropriate for different types of learning scenarios

- comprehend legal issues and other problems related to the use of music

Training with a Beat: The Teaching Power of Music is divided into three sections: defining the why, what, and how of music.

1. "Music Explored" examines why music helps people learn.

2. "Music Explained" addresses what music is.

3. "Music Applied" focuses on how to use music in learning situations.

Music Explored

"Music Explored" establishes the framework for our exploration of the musical beat. It examines underlying factors that will become useful in later chapters and discovers the connection between human and musical origins.

In chapter 1, "Music and You," we will examine the personal relationship between human beings and music, discover the pervasiveness of music in today's world, and discuss the multitude of effects music has on us.

Chapter 2, "The Birth of Music," explores the beginnings of our musical heritage. It examines the ways in which music and language may have intertwined at the beginning, and, in so doing, it will help us begin our exploration of the teaching power of music.

Chapter 3, "The Triune Brain," discusses Paul MacLean's theory of human brain evolution, an evolution that may have coincided with the development of music. MacLean's theory offers possible explanations for music's ability to move us both emotionally and intellectually.

In chapter 4, "Left Right Left," we build on the work of Roger Sperry. The discussion examines the difference between the brain's left and right hemispheres. We will explore ways in which the left hemisphere's rationality and the right hemisphere's creativity partner to hear and enjoy music.

Brain waves are the subject of chapter 5, "Brain Vibrations." The cycle time of the brain's waves plays an important function in our daily lives and is one of the sources of music's teaching power. We will discover how the good vibrations emanating from a person's brain respond to music, encouraging learning.

Chapter 6, "Musical Intelligence," uses both Howard Gardner's Multiple Intelligences and Daniel Goleman's Emotional Intelligences theories as departure points for two discussions: music's function as a core intelligence and music's emotionality and the importance of harnessing emotions while training.

Chapter 7, "Music and Learning," discusses the effectiveness of learning throughout human history, looking for trends, factors, and other specifics that help establish basic guidelines for training with a beat.

Music Explained

The next section, "Music Explained," provides a layperson's explanation of musical theory. It avoids lengthy theoretical discussions and instead focuses on information a trainer requires to intelligently select training music.

Chapter 8, "The Musical Pulse," examines pulse, rhythm, beat, and meter. It explains, in the clearest terms possible, what different meters are and what those distinctions mean for the training beat.

The difference between sound and music and a definition of when a sound actually becomes music are the foci of chapter 9, "The Musical Sound." An overview of musical terminology required for training placement is offered.

Chapter 10, "Musical Styles," explores genres of music available to trainers. It begins the process of applying music to the classroom, providing a lengthy but clear explanation of classical music, as well as other genres, leading toward an understanding of effective music placement within training activities.

Music Applied

"Music Applied" is the final section. It gets to the heart of musical training, offering explanations, examples, and tools for harnessing the teaching power of music.

Chapter 11, "Teaching with Music," relates specific examples of music placement, along with a series of guidelines for the learning principles involved. A continuing vignette of one trainer's struggles while teaching diversity to a reluctant audience provides additional insight into the musical-training process.

Chapter 12, "Teaching with Lyrics," explores the important aspects of lyrical music. Songs with lyrics, although extremely effective, require a separate set of parameters. This chapter offers simple rules based on those guidelines.

Chapter 13, "Musical Precautions," discusses the potential pitfalls of teaching with music. Among the subjects explored are participant expectations, cost, technical problems, and legal issues.

Chapter 14, "Training with a Beat," brings the discussion to a close with some final observations about the teaching power of music.

ろ

In addition to the many chapters, vignettes occur throughout the book. These stories provide additional insight while placing the discussion within a personal context. They are works of fiction, with no intentional representation of any event, location, or person, living or dead.

Finally, a series of appendices provides the reader with helpful additional resources and information. These appendices include:

- a glossary that defines key terms used throughout the book

- a listing of the "Music Notes" placed throughout the book. These music notes summarize key learning points and offer guidelines for music placement.

- a listing of classical music resources available to trainers

- a compilation of other music resources, including retailers, recording companies, and Internet sites

- a music placement matrix, providing a resource for selecting music appropriate for different situations

- an index of key information contained within the book

Perhaps the most valuable appendix is the one that provides three different pop placement listings. Recordings from the last fifty years of popular music have been cross-referenced in three different ways:

- by artist, with each artist and their song listed alphabetically
- by song title, with each selection and the artist who recorded it listed alphabetically
- by learning function, with songs grouped according to their possible usage. Some of the topics included are change, career development, communications, diversity, leadership, sexual harassment, time management, and technical training.

These three comprehensive listings provide trainers, teachers, and facilitators with a critical reference from which to effectively select popular songs appropriate to different situations.

I hope this book will help you discover the effectiveness of music as a learning tool. And in the process, may you discover your beat.

Part One

MUSIC

Explained

Explored

Applied

Music is edifying, for from time to time
it sets the soul in operation.

—John Cage

Chapter 1

MUSIC AND YOU

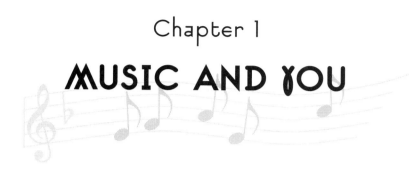

Going to the Chapel

"I can't go through with this," I shiver. Through frosted glass, I can see the results of last night's blizzard. Everything, including the mountain, is covered in white. It looks so cold, so forlorn, not at all like the day I met Tommy.

Sharon and I, celebrating my homecoming, had gone to Hofner's Seventy-Five Lanes. A bowling alley seems an odd place to meet your future husband, but in small mountain communities, establishments function in many ways. Hofner's was more than a bowling alley. It was also the town's best restaurant and lounge and the local gathering place. I had just completed my nursing degree and chose to return home, accepting a position at the Wilson Elderly Home.

I was not looking for, nor expecting to meet, anyone, but the moment Tommy looked my way, I knew I had found my reason for returning to Saranac Lake. Tommy and I talked for hours. Sharon, ever the true friend, faded away in spite of our plans. It seemed like only minutes when Hofner's closed for the night. Neither Tommy nor I were ready to part. Instead, we drove up the mountain and watched the springtime sun rise over the mountain peak. It was our dawn. The promise of it was reflected in our eyes.

But now, looking through this frozen window, the sun is hidden. The mountain has turned cold. "I can hide out there," I think, "in my white gown; they'd never find me."

"What's wrong, baby?" Dad asks in panic, while glancing sideways at Sharon.

"Tommy would be a wonderful husband, but still . . . I don't know, . . . I'm so nervous."

*Dad, to calm my nerves, pours me a shot of brandy. I gulp it down, choke on its dryness, and cough on my gown. "Quick," I say, "bring Tommy in here. Let him see the real me. Maybe **he'll** call it off."*

A strange smile suddenly crosses Sharon's face. "Everyone's waiting," she says hurriedly, "and I have to go to the choir loft." Sharon had volunteered to play organ for the ceremony. It was to be her wedding gift. "When I start playing, I promise you will know this is the right thing to do." With that, she left. The few minutes it took her to reach the loft seemed like an eternity, but finally the organ bellowed to life.

"Wait," I thought. "That song! It was playing when I first saw Tommy." As Sharon and I had entered Hofner's that night, there, across the room, stood Tommy, looking at me. God, he was handsome. I remember leaning toward Sharon, leveling a finger at Tommy, and with all-knowing assuredness, shouting over the music, "I'll marry him someday." So odd, those words were in the song, and the song said them the moment I did. Sharon and I had looked at each other surprised. We both laughed at the coincidence. And now, she was playing that song; a

*reminder from an old friend. Of course I will marry Tommy. I knew it the
first time I saw him looking at me and the jukebox played our song.*

> Music is so naturally united with us that we
> cannot be free from it even if we so desired.
> —Boethius[1]

Music is woven into the fabric of our lives. It is in your home, on
your television, in the movies, in your car, on the elevator, at the store,
at your work site, in the doctor's office, and in the nightclub. People
everywhere work, drive, eat, sleep, dream, and make love to music.
Music is our friend, our confidant, our companion.

Musicologist Richard Norton described the situation aptly when
he stated:

> There is no form of popular music in the modern, industrialized
> world that exists outside the province of mass tonal consciousness. It
> is the tonality of the church, school, office, parade, convention, cafe-
> teria, workplace, airport, airplane, automobile, truck, tractor, lounge,
> lobby, bar, gym, brothel, bank, and elevator. Afraid of being without
> it while on foot, humans are presently strapping it to their bodies in
> order to walk to it, run to it, work to it, and relax to it. It is every-
> where.[2]

Although today's technology allows for this continuous attachment,
the phenomenon is not a recent development. Music has performed an
important role in every known civilization, past and present. Most
societies mark the important stages of a person's life with specific types
or pieces of music. There are birth songs, birthday songs, coming-of-
age songs, graduation songs, anniversary songs, holiday songs, retire-
ment songs, and even death songs. Music's influence is so prevalent
that, to this day, most of us remember songs that played at our most
important moments.

Even if music were banned, the soundtrack would continue. Music is not an external event, it is in our heads and hearts. It is our comforter, our soul mate. Kendall Walton, in his essay "Listening with Imagination," states, "I feel intimate with the music. It is as though I am inside the music, or it is inside me."[3] Music's intimacy is so powerful that it seduces us. In fact, the German philosopher Friedrich Nietzsche described the relationship as one of seduction:

> This is what happens to us in music. First one has to *learn to hear* a figure and melody at all, to detect and distinguish it, to isolate it and delimit it as a separate life. Then it requires some exertion and good will to *tolerate* it in spite of its strangeness, to be patient with its appearance and expression, and kindhearted about its oddity. Finally there comes a moment when we are used to it, when we wait for it, when we sense that we should miss it if it were missing; and now it continues to compel and enchant us relentlessly until we have become its humble and enraptured lovers who desire nothing better from the world than it and only it.[4]

I believe, like Nietzsche, that music seduces, and that the seduction is both individual and universal. Music is interpretative enough to be communally understood, yet personal and intimate enough to share our deepest thoughts. Simon Frith explains, "because of its qualities of abstractness music is an individualizing form. We absorb songs into our lives and rhythms into our bodies; they have a looseness of reference that makes them immediately accessible."[5] Music crawls into every fiber of our being, becoming one with us and affecting our lives in many ways:

- Music affects shopping habits.
- Music affects mood.
- Music affects productivity.
- Music affects health.

Music Mind News

All the news your mind needs!

Language Related to Music

Patel found related brain potentials during the processing of linguistic and musical structural relations, suggesting that structural integration processes in speech and music may share neural resources.

Working For a Living

People reported to Blood and Ferriss that their conversations were more satisfying when music was playing in the background, increasing their productivity while lowering their anxiety levels.

I Get Some Satisfaction

Dimensions of Critical Care Nursing reports that intensive care patients who listen to music reduce their blood pressure and score higher on emotional wellness tests.

The Surgery Serenade

Miluk-Kolasa and colleagues measured cortisol levels in patients in conjunction with informing them that they undergo surgery the next day. The patients who listened to music experienced reduced levels of anxiety.

Don't Worry About a Thing

A team headed by Escher selected a group of patients undergoing gastroscopy. The patients listened to the type of music they preferred. The patients exhibited significantly lower levels of stress hormone.

Whistle While You Shop

Milliman studied the effectiveness of music in a national chain of supermarkets and found that the use of slow music increased sales more than the use of fast music. The length of shopper stay expanded, and more items were purchased, ranging in increased sales from $12,112.35 per store to $16,740.23; a gain of 39.2 percent.

Shop Till Ya Drop

According to Timmerman, people felt less crowded in shopping situations when background music was present.

Pump It Up

Music that builds through a repeating fifteen minute cycle, has been proven to help people pay attention and focus on the tasks at hand.

Muzak to Their Ears

The Muzak Corporation reported that sales to shoppers under twenty-five increased 51 percent, twenty-six to fifty rose 11 percent, and over fifty, 26 percent when music was present.

Walking in Rhythm

One supermarket found that grocery sales increased 28 percent when people walked in rhythm with the slower pace of moderate tempo music. Slower instrumental music was found to be most effective in a dining setting, encouraging people to drink an average of three more beverages per table.

Music Mind News references in order of appearance top to bottom.

1. Patel, A.D., Gibson, E., Ratner, J., Besson, M., Holcomb, P.J. "Processing Syntactic Relations in Language and Music: an event-related potential study," *The Journal of Cognitive Neuroscience,* 1998, Nov. 10 (6): 717–33.

2. Blood, D.J., and Ferriss, S.J., "Effects of Background Music on Anxiety, Satisfaction with Communication, and Productivity," *Psychological Reports, 72/1* (1993): 171–77.

3. Updike, P., "Music Therapy Results for ICU Patients," *Dimensions of Critical Care Nursing, 9* (1990): 39–45.

4. Miluk-Kolasa, B., Obminski, S., Stupnicki, R., and Golec, L., "Effects of Music Treatment on Salivary Cortisol in Patients Exposed to Pre-surgical Stress, *Experimental and Clinical Endocrinology, 102,* (1994): 118–120.

5. Escher, J., Hohmann, U., Anthenien, L., Dayer, E., Bosshard, C., and Gaillard, R.C., "Schweizerische Medizinische Wochenschrift," *Journal Suisse de Medecine,* 1998, Nov. 10 (6): 717–33.

6. Milliman, R.E., "Using Background Music to Affect the Behavior of Supermarket Shoppers," *Journal of Marketing,* 46 (1982): 86–92.

7. Timmerman, J. E. "The Effects of Temperature, Music, and Density on the Perception of Crowding and Shopping Behavior of Consumers in a Retail Environment," *DAI,* 42-03A (1981): 11293.

8. Huron, D., "The Ramp Archetype and the Maintenance of Passive Auditory Attention," *Music Perception,* 10/1 (1992): 83–91.

9. "Business Music: a merchandising tool for the retail industry," Seattle: Muzak Corporation, 1991.

10. Ibid.

Music Affects Shopping Habits

"Elevator" music exists because of its effectiveness. People feel less crowded and less stressed in shopping situations when background music is present.[6] Proper selection of music translates into higher profitability. The use of slow music increases sales. The use of slow (adagio) Baroque music can increase sales by as much as 38 percent![7]

Music Affects Mood

Music can calm, relax, excite, motivate to action, and otherwise suggest appropriate emotions to people.[8] When music excites us, for instance, our blood pressure and heartbeat rise, our bodies focus, and our muscles tense; we become aroused.[9] The power to heal frail emotions, or calm a sick body, are beneficial effects of music.

This power is also valuable as a persuasion tool. Movie sound tracks are the ultimate example of manipulation through music. Often, every movie situation, activity, or emotion has a corresponding musical theme. Movie music is designed to bring forth the appropriate emotions within your mind. The next time you watch a favorite movie, listen to the sound track. Next, imagine that same movie without its music. Better yet, play some completely different background music as you watch the film. Suddenly, the terrifying movie with the creepy music will seem comical, or romantic, or full of energy. In this way, you will discover the importance of music to the movie experience.

Music Affects Productivity

The mind and body instinctually fall into rhythm with the beat of music. All sorts of routine tasks—such as jogging, sewing, hiking, and driving—are more successful when music accompanies the activity. Assembly line efficiency improves when background music is linked to repeated motion at appropriate speeds. A whole culture of music derived from the work chants that African-American slaves used in the fields while picking the "Massa's" cotton. The slaves would use their rhythmic singsong tradition to build a sense of community. Music, when timed to the field work, made the labor easier, while spreading information, sharing emotions, and warning of approaching danger. In the words of B. B. King, "The blues could warn you what was coming. I could see the blues was about survival."[10]

Music Affects Health

Music can alter the human body's physiology, making people happier, healthier, and smarter; helping the body fight off viruses; reducing stress hormone levels; and affecting the heartbeat, pulse rate, and blood pressure. People about to undergo surgery have experienced shorter recovery times after listening to enjoyable music,[11] while patients in group therapy have more open discussion when music is present.[12]

Some non-Western cultures certainly believe in the healing power of music. The Navajo Indians believe special songs are so valuable for healing that knowledge of those songs is considered wealth.[13] The Temia people of Malaysia regard music's primary purpose to be for healing rituals.[14] Similar beliefs are held worldwide by people of different cultures, religions, and traditions.

Music Note 1

Music has numerous effects on people:
♪ Music affects shopping habits.
♪ Music affects mood.
♪ Music affects productivity.
♪ Music affects health.

These claims for the effectiveness of music, although documented, seem fantastic. What's going on here? How could all this be possible? In our next chapter, we will explore the birth of music. Discovering music's origin may help us comprehend why music reaches so deeply into our being.

Notes

1. Boethius, A., quoted by Ehrich, E., and De Bruhl, M. (1996). *The International Thesaurus of Quotations*. New York: HarperCollins Publishers, Inc.

2. Norton, R. (1984). *Tonality in Western Culture*. University Park: Pennsylvania State University Press.

3. Walton, K. (1997). "Listening with Imagination" *Music and Meaning*. Jenefer Robinson, ed. Ithaca, N.Y.: Cornell University Press.

4. Nietzsche, F. (1974). *The Gay Science: with a prelude in rhymes and an appendix of songs*, trans. W. Kaufmann. New York: Random House.

5. Frith, S. (1987). "Towards an Aesthetic of Popular Music." *Music and Society: the politics of composition, performance, and perception*. Richard Leppert and Susan McClary, eds. Cambridge, U.K.: Cambridge University Press.

6. Stratton, V. N. "Influence of Music and Socializing on Perceived Stress while Waiting." *Perceptual and Motor Skills*, 75/1 (1992): 334; Timmerman, J. E. "The Effects of Temperature, Music, and Density on the Perception of Crowding and Shopping Behavior of Consumers in a Retail Environment." *DAI*, 42/03A (1981): 1293.

7. Muzak Corporation. (1991). *Business Music: a merchandising tool for the retail industry*, quoted by Campbell, D. (1997). *The Mozart Effect*. New York: Avon Books.

8. Pignatiello, M., Camp, C., Elder, S., and Rasar, L. "A Psychophysiological Comparison of the Velten and Musical Mood Induction Techniques." *Journal of Music Therapy*, 26/3 (1989): 140–54; Tergwot, M. M., and van Grinsven, F. "Musical Expression of Mood States." *Psychology of Music*, 19 (1991): 99–109; Thaut, M., and de l'Etoile, S., "The Effects of Music on Mood State-Dependent Recall." *Journal of Music Therapy*, 30/2 (1993): 70–80; North, A., and Hargreaves, D. "Liking, Arousal Potential, and the Emotions Expressed by Music." *Scandinavian Journal of Psychology*, 38 (1997): 45–53; Jensen, K. "The Effects of Selected Classical Music on Writing and Talking about Significant Life Events." *DAI*, 56/12A (1995): 4602.

9. Storr, A. (1992). *Music and the Mind*. New York: Random House, Inc.

10. King, B.B., and Ritz, D. (1999). *Blues All Around Me: the autobiography of B.B. King*. New York: Morrow.

11. McGaugh, J., and Cahill, L. "Music during Gastroscopy." *Schweizerische Medizinische Wochenschrift*, 123 (1982): 1354–58; Miluk-Kolasa, B., Obminski, S., Stupnicki, R., and Golec, L. "Effects of Music Treatment on Salivary Cortisol in Patients Exposed to Pre-surgical Stress." *Experimental and Clinical Endocrinology*, 102 (1994): 118–20.

12. Stewart, D. "The Sound Link: psychodynamic group music therapy in a therapeutic setting." *Psychoanalytic Psychotherapy*, 11 (1997): 29–46.

13. McAllester, D. "Enemy Way Music: a study of social and esthetic values as seen in navaho music," papers of the Peabody Museum of American Archaeology and Ethnology, Harvard University, Cambridge: Peabody Museum (1954): 66.

14. Roseman, M. (1991). *Healing Sounds from the Malaysian Rainforest: Temiar music and medicine*. Berkeley and Los Angeles: University of California Press.

Chapter 2

THE BIRTH OF MUSIC

The Healer of the Cave

The child was ill. It would be gone before the sun. There were no doctors, no science, no medicine, or drugs, or at least what we think of when we talk about science, or medicine, or drugs. There was one hope: the healer of the cave. The healer led the clan in worship—homages to the gods, prayers for protection against the beasts, and celebrations of the hunt. The child's mother entered the cave, one arm holding the child, the other holding a torch. It was a long walk down the dank corridor. As she traveled deep into the cave, she saw walls covered with paintings. Some atoned to the gods, others celebrated the return of the waters, still others prayed for healing.

Finally, she reached the worship place. The healer glanced up, the fire casting an eerie glow on his face. She acknowledged him with a bow and a grunt. Language was primitive, just a few sounds—a combination of *birdsong, animal roar, and chant. People in the Cro-Magnon age had not yet mastered language, but the healer had a special talent: he could make pleasing sounds with his voice.*

With a wave of the clan's totem over the child, the ceremony began. The totem cast an eerie, larger than life, almost godlike shadow on the walls. The healer held the child and began to dance and chant. If sounds in this cave were heard by the gods, the woman now understood why. The chant reverberated from wall to wall. The sound was so full... so... "godly"; it enveloped her with its richness. This cave sounded god-like because, of all the caves, this one had the best acoustics. Her brain would not understand the science of the event, even if someone in that age, thirty thousand years ago, had the capability of explaining it. All she knew was that the gods would hear this song.

> There is evidence that early human species were able to dance and sing several hundred thousand years before homo sapiens emerged with the capacity for speech as we now know it.[1]
>
> —John Blacking

No one knows who created the first music. No one. Recorded musical history begins around the time of ancient Greece and the Roman empire. The earliest records we have come from forty or so fragments of Greek music. No ancient Roman music survives. Written accounts, bas-reliefs, mosaics, paintings, and sculptures do, however, suggest that music was central to Roman military life, theater, religion, and ritual.[2] The oldest documented "popular" songs are Latin from the eleventh and twelfth centuries B.C. These songs revolved around three themes that remain popular to this day: wine, women, and satire. The first musical tome, *On Music,* by the Christian church leader St. Augustine, was written around 387 A.D.[3] By that time, music must have had a real presence. The work is six volumes long, indicating that plenty of information about music was available for discussion.

But, what of music's origin? Where did it come from? Who were the first musical talents? Even without documentation, some intelligent guesses are possible. It is highly likely that music existed before language. The need for higher levels of communication may have, over time, necessitated that our ancestors speak, with language evolving from the music. Archaeological proof of this hypothesis exists. Ancient cave drawings often include depictions of people dancing. Remnants of musical instruments dating back thirty thousand years have been discovered.[4] Artifacts recovered from caves include primitive percussion instruments and bone flutes.[5]

Another clue comes from language itself. Many cultures have no separate words for music and language.[6] In the ancient Greek language, any word for artful speech included a musical connotation. *Melos*, for instance, is the Greek word for both lyric poetry and music. Early languages, almost without exception, were chanted. They were melodic and poetic, not dry and practical.[7] It is highly likely that music was the original language.

Music Note 2

> *Music may be the original language.*

Remnants of this melodic tradition still exist in vocal inflection. Political speeches, teaching, and popular music are but a few examples.

- Ronald Reagan, Martin Luther King Jr., Winston Churchill, and Margaret Thatcher were excellent communicators whose ability to soar with their voice drove their success.

- Teachers often vary their vocal tone while lecturing to keep learners alert and emphasize key words and concepts. Students certainly recognize this fact. One of their most common complaints is about teachers who lecture in a monotone.

- Rap music is perhaps the best modern example of melodic speech. The rapper must convey melodic content without singing. To the casual listener, it sounds as if anyone could rap. Record sales disprove that notion.

How Music Began

This information helps us comprehend the connection between language and music, but it leaves us with the question of how music itself began. Four schools of thought seem prevalent. Music may have begun as a way of:

- communicating with God
- joining together
- attracting a mate
- expressing love
- communicating between adults and infants

Music Began as a Way of Communicating with God

Early humans with a gift for vocalizations may have gained attention by singing. Other group members, awed by those vocal mutterings, could have regarded them as a supernatural gift. When combined with the echoing acoustics of cave dwellings, this effect would have been doubly impressive. In fact, archeologists have discovered that caves with the most primitive wall paintings tend to have the best acoustics.[8] Clan members might have regarded these early vocalists as a link to their gods—singing for healing, good fortune, and thanksgiving. "Vocal music may have begun as a special way of communicating with the supernatural; a way which shared many of the features of ordinary speech, but which was also distinctive."[9]

History does suggest that music has always had a spiritual connection:[10]

- The very word "music" comes from the Greek word *mousikos*, meaning "of the muses" (the Greek goddesses who inspired poets, painters, musicians, and so forth). Both The *Iliad* and *Odyssey* feature songs, dirges, and hymns of praise to Apollo.[11] The Greeks regarded music as having a divine origin, being invented by the gods. They believed it could heal, purify, and work miracles and that it penetrated the soul.[12]

- In India, ragas are perceived to express certain moods or emotions; some are believed to personify gods, and some are perceived as having great power.[13]

- In many African religions, sound is thought to be one of the primary means by which deities and humans impose order on the universe. In west Africa, drummers play a crucial role in possession-trance ceremonies. A competent drummer must know scores of specific rhythms for particular gods and is responsible for regulating the flow of supernatural power in ritual contexts.[14]

- Early Christians believed the value of music lay in its ability to inspire good and evil. Christian church leaders feared the evil power of music so much that they contemplated banning all music to suppress Roman pagan ritual traditions. Fortunately, the inspiration music provided was too powerful. The idea was abandoned so as to not lose all music.[15]

Music Began as a Way of Joining Together

In many cultures, music is valued as a way of coming together and joining around shared values and beliefs. Some American Indian tribes, in a view shared by some Asian and African societies, believe that music mirrors cosmic harmonies and that by making music, a group can increase the harmony between a community and the universe.[16] Our modern society hints at these beliefs. For many people, music is a central feature of concerts, sporting events, festivals, and other communal events.

Music Began as a Way of Attracting a Mate

British naturalist Charles Darwin hypothesized that individual species members best able to thrive in their environment survive and multiply, while those less strong perish.[17] Darwin also suggested a musical connection to survival. "The suspicion does not appear improbable that the progenitors of man, either males of females, or both sexes, before they acquired the power of expressing their mutual love in articulate language, endeavored to charm each other with musical tones and rhythm."[18]

In *The Origins of Music,* biomusicology professor Bjorn Merker expands that theme, suggesting that music came about for sex and the continuation of the human species. Dr. Merker studied chimpanzee group behavior as an indicator of how our ancestors might have used vocal sounds. He discovered that chimps "sing" to attract mates. As protection against inbreeding, female chimps instinctively leave their own group to seek out a mate from a different group. Male vocalizations provide an auditory road map for the female as she searches for the other males. Male chimps, to create greater volume and increase their chances of being heard, vocalize in groups. So, evolutionary pressures may have forced male chimps to sing together, helping females find their mates.[19]

Music Began as a Way of Expressing Love

Another view is that love, not sex, was the inspiration for music. Humans might have transcended instinctual brain behavior only when individual couples began expressing love for each other, and those expressions of love may have become the beginnings of language.[20] As we will see in chapter 3, this idea parallels Paul MacLean's Triune Brain theory. The need to express emotion may have furthered the development of the limbic system, as our ancestors evolved past their primitive reptilian system.

Music Began as a Way of Communicating between Adults and Infants

Have you ever talked to a baby? Did what you said make sense? How about the contour of your voice? Were the pitches you used within your normal range? Did you notice yourself speaking in a singsong form?

When we talk to infants, our faces take on different expressions, as do our voices. We restrict our pitch to a limited range and rhythmic pattern, and our sounds to repeated cooing and babbling.[21] If you talked to adults that way, they would think you were insane. Yet, amazingly, the baby responds, and you instinctively do more of what the baby responds to, and less of what it ignores.

This phenomenon occurs the world over. Studies confirm that children's lullabies, regardless of culture or locale,[22] have many of these same characteristics, with simple pitch contours and repeated rhythms.[23]

It may be that language started this way, with a mother trying to reach her child, and the child responding. As this adult-infant communication evolved, it may have become language or song. The simplicity of the communication makes it possible that these cooings were the first spoken words, as infant and adult learned to talk together.

Music Note 3

Music may have begun as a way of:
♪ communicating with God
♪ joining together
♪ attracting a mate
♪ expressing love
♪ communicating between adults and infants

I believe all four theories have merit, perhaps in combination. However it happened, it is apparent that our ancestors used songs to survive, procreate, communicate, nurture, and learn. As the human brain evolved, music may have receded into the background, leaving spoken word as our language. Even though the primacy of music faded, it still communicates feelings and establishes community among individuals. It is an ancient universal language that transcends words. That transcendence gives music its power as a teaching tool. At its root, the beat of humanity is music.

Notes

1. Blacking, J. (1987). *A Commonsense View of All Music.* Cambridge, U.K.: Cambridge University Press.

2. Grout, D. J., and Palisca, C. (1996). *A History of Western Music,* 5th ed. New York: W.W. Norton & Company.

3. Ibid.

4. *The 1995 Grolier Multimedia Encyclopedia.* (1995). vr. 7.0.2. Grolier Electronic Publishing, Inc.

5. Bruney, C. (1935). *A General History of Music from the Earliest Ages to the Present Period.* London: Oxford University Press.

6. Storr, A. (1992). *Music and the Mind.* New York: Random House, Inc.

7. Cranston, M. (1983). *Jean-Jacques.* London: Allen Lane.

8. Jourdain, R. (1997). *Music, the Brain, and Ecstasy: how music captures our imagination.* New York: Avon Books.

9. Nettl, B. (1983). *The Study of Ethnomusicology.* Urbana and Chicago: University of Illinois Press.

10. Grout, D. J., and Palisca, C. (1996).

11. Ibid.

12. Ibid.

13. *The 1995 Grolier Multimedia Encyclopedia.* (1995).

14. Ibid.

15. Grout, D. J., and Palisca, C. (1996).

16. *The 1995 Grolier Multimedia Encyclopedia.* (1995).

17. Darwin, C. (1859). *On the Origin of Species.* London: John Murray.

18. Storr, A. (1992).

19. Merker, B. (1999). "Synchronous Chorusing and Human Origins." *The Origins of Music.* Wallin, N., Merker, B., and Brown, S., eds. Cambridge, Massachusetts: MIT Press.

20. Money, J. "Evolutionary Sexology: the hypothesis of song and sex." *Medical Hypotheses,* 48 (1997): 399–402.

21. Stern, D. N., Spieker, S., and MacKain, K. "Intonation Contours as Signals in Maternal Speech to Prelinguistic Infants." *Developmental Psychology,* 18 (1982): 727–735.

22. Jacobson, J., Boersma, D., Fields, R., and Olson, K. "Paralinguistic Features of Speech to Infants and Small Children." *Child Development,* 54 (1993): 436–442.

23. Weinberger, N. M. Musica Research Notes, II/1 (Spring 1995). <www.musica.uci.edu>.

Chapter 3

THE TRIUNE BRAIN

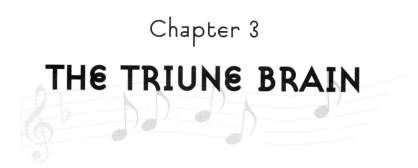

Revolution

"5 . . . 4 . . . 3 . . . 2 . . . 1 . . . , camera one, you're on."

"Hello. My name is Fran Frank. Welcome back to News *at Nine. As we told you before the last break, the Evolution Dogs were in town tonight. Our roving reporter, John Franklin, is at the arena now. John. John. Can you hear me?"*

"Yes, Fran, it's a little noisy, but I can hear you."

"Tell us, John, what's going on now?"

"Well, Fran, the concert just ended and fans are pouring out of the arena."

"Did they enjoy the concert?"

"It appears so, but let's ask the fans.

"Here comes one now, and, judging by his appearance, he's been a fan since the sixties. Sir, how was the concert?"

"Man, they rocked! It was like 3-D sound. There were speakers in front of us, to the left, to the right; they were everywhere. I could feel the sound vibrating through the floor and up my spine. My chest pounded so hard, I thought it'd punch a hole in it. It was awesome!"

"Ah, Fran, that fan certainly enjoyed the concert, . . . or something."

"Yes, he sure did."

"Here's another one, a teenager. Excuse me . . . ."

"Heather, like my name is Heather."

"Heather, how was the concert?"

"Moving. When Larry Limbic sang about the lonely people, I cried. It's like the best thing that's ever happened to me. I'll remember tonight forever. LARRY! LARRY LIMBIC! IF YOU'RE WATCHING, I LOVE YOU!!!"

"Thank you."

"We have time for one more."

"What, Fran?"

"We have time for one more."

"Sorry, that was right in my ear. Fran, here's an older fan's opinion for you. Sir, did you enjoy the concert?"

"The Evolution Dogs's lineup of lead guitar, bass guitar, double keyboards, percussion, and synthesized sounds is always interesting. Their music is well thought through. The progression of material was logical, starting with their first hit and progressing methodically through each of their hits. My only complaint is that some of their lyrics aren't thought through. But all in all, I would say the event was well presented."

"Thank you, sir. Well, there you have it, Fran. Three very different fans, three very different opinions, all positive. I'd say it was a good night for the Evolution Dogs. Back to you, Fran."

"Thanks, John. Coming up next is Paul MacLean, right after this message...."

"And we're off."

Sound is an experience a brain extracts from its environment.

—Robert Jourdain[1]

Without the human brain, there could be no music. Animals make melodious sounds, but cannot, at will, repeat exact prolonged and varying sequences. They have no capacity for the abstract thinking required to unify sounds over time. Only the human brain can organize sounds into moving compositions and then re-create those sounds at will. Our ability to think makes it possible for us to understand music in a way that is incomprehensible to animals. It is one of the miracles of humanity.

The process by which this miracle occurs is as obscure as is the origin of music itself, but thanks to the hard work of researchers, a basic understanding is possible. That knowledge will help us apply the teaching power of music.

> We carry our evolution inside us, within the
> different structures of the brain, structures
> built in different eras.
>
> —Robert Ornstein and David S. Sobel[2]

The noted brain researcher Dr. Paul MacLean[3] proposed that the human brain actually has three layers, developed over thousands and thousands of years. Our ancestors' original brain was an extremely primitive instinctual brain. Eventually, an emotional component encircled it. Finally, a logical brain grew to engulf the other two. MacLean called this theory the "triune brain."

Metaphorically, the three brains look somewhat like a wrapped lollipop. The stick represents the first brain, the stem. It performs only basic tasks, providing essential support for the lollipop. The lollipop itself represents the second brain, the center of emotions. This brain separates things that feel good from those that do not, even though it does not exactly know what "good" means. The wrapper around the lollipop represents the intellectual brain, applying thought and reason to the situation. It is logical to cover the lollipop; the wrapper prevents the spread of disease, preserves the candy, and provides a place to display the lollipop's ingredients and nutritional value. Whereas the first brain provides basic functions and the second brain responds emotionally, the third brain reasons intellectually.

The Triune Brain

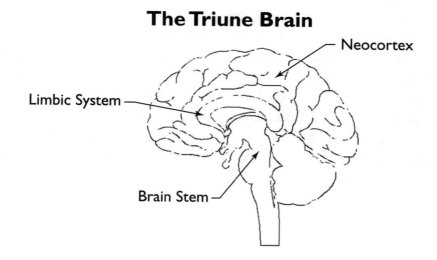

Neocortex

Limbic System

Brain Stem

Triune Responsibilities

	Reptilian	Limbic	Neocortex
Function	Ancient, primitive brain emerging out of our spinal column and driven by instinct	Center of the emotions, assigning appropriate levels of emotion	Home of logic, enabling rational thought
Controls	Breathing, pulse and heart rate	Hormones, thirst, hunger, sexuality, the body's pleasure centers, metabolism, the autonomic nervous system, and portions of long-term memory	Hearing, vision, language, and all higher-level functioning
Response to Music	Sorts incoming sound, determining direction, volume, threat potential	Reacts to music emotionally, selecting appropriate emotive responses	Responds to music intellectually, analyzing it, and placing it into a context for understanding

The Reptilian Brain

Dr. MacLean described the original brain, our "lollipop stick," as the ancient, primitive reptilian brain that emerges out of our spinal column. This brain is driven by instinct. Lizards, birds, and alligators rely on it. The reptilian brain controls your breathing, your pulse and heart rate, and your instincts, such as the tendency to fight or flee during potentially dangerous situations. When danger presents itself, "the human brain is downshifted to the more primitive areas of the brain. We revert to instinctual behavior rather than use rational judgment."[4] Fortunately, it is not our only source of brainpower.

The reptilian brain is one mechanism our bodies use to absorb sound. In the brain stem, the auditory nerve connects with the muscles of your body. Sounds enter your body not just through the ear, but also through your nerve endings,[5] moving to the spinal cord and into your brain. If you have ever attended a concert and felt a sub-woofer thumping in your chest, you have experienced these kind of vibrations. Even babies in the womb "hear" sounds through the vibrations of the mother's voice.[6]

The brain stem focuses its attention on all incoming sound. Because of its limited firepower, this brain confines itself to sorting sounds—determining what direction a sound is coming from, how loud the sound is, and the potential threat represented by the sound. The brain stem's job is not to hear each note, but to identify and organize notes so that your other brains can recognize them as music.[7] It is a traffic light, stuck on green, allowing information through without regard for the comparative importance of each piece of information.

The Limbic System (Paleomammalian)

> Music is feeling, then, not sound.
> —Wallace Stevens[8]

Dr. MacLean proposed that a second brain, the limbic, or mammalian brain, grew over and encircled our ancestors' reptilian brains. If the reptilian brain is a nonjudgmental traffic light, the limbic brain is a computerized traffic control system, responding to the emotional impact the sound represents. The limbic system is the center of the emotions. This brain "feels" signals it receives from the brain stem and assigns appropriate levels of emotion. Depending on the signals it receives, the limbic system can make you angry, scared, happy, or sad. This brain is the one that causes us to lash out during emotional moments.

The limbic system responds to music emotionally. It senses the feeling within the song, welling the corresponding emotion up within us. In the words of composer Franz Liszt:

> If music has one advantage, [it is its] supreme capacity to make each inner impulse audible without the assistance of reason. Reason, after all, is restricted in the diversity of its means and is capable only of confirming or describing our affections, not of communicating them

directly in their full intensity. . . . Music, on the other hand, presents at once the intensity and the expression of *feeling*. It is the embodied and intelligible essence of feeling, capable of being apprehended by our senses. It permeates them like a dart, like a ray, like a mist, like a spirit, and fills our soul.[9]

This ability to capture our emotions is a major source of music's learning power. It alone would make our limbic system important, but the limbic system does much more. It also controls your hormones, thirst, hunger, sexuality; your body's pleasure centers; your metabolism; your autonomic nervous system; and, most important, portions of your long-term memory.[10]

The limbic system acts as the long-term memory's gatekeeper, allowing some but not all incoming information to enter.[11] Benign or somewhat painful memories get repressed, but information with strong positive (or negative) emotional content receives a green light through the limbic system and passes into long-term memory.[12] Dr. James McGaugh describes this process as follows: "We believe that the brain takes advantage of the chemicals released during stress and powerful emotions to regulate the strength of storage of the memory."[13] If you remember the day your child was born, the day you graduated from school, or the day you received that big promotion, you have had this experience.

The learning importance of this effect cannot be overstated. When trainees are having emotionally pleasant experiences in your classroom, their own brains may help you increase their learning.

Music Note 4

If trainees are having emotionally pleasant experiences in your classroom, their learning may increase.

The Neocortex (Neomammalian)

Music is the art of thinking with sound.
—Jules Combarie[14]

Over the limbic system is your neocortex, which in ancient Latin meant "bark."[15] This brain, wrapping around the other two brains, is by far the largest of the three. Flattened out, the neocortex would equal the size of two twelve-inch pizzas, one on each side of your head.[16] The neocortex is your thinking brain. It is the home of logic, enabling us to reason, hear, think, and speak. The neocortex absorbs all those sounds your reptilian brain and the limbic system send its way and organizes them into a coherent whole, into music.

Music Note 5

The human brain has three layers. Each hears music in its own way:
♪ The reptilian brain hears sound as vibration.
♪ The limbic system hears sound as feeling.
♪ The neocortex hears sound intellectually.

Dr. MacLean has been accused of oversimplifying the brain's processes, but his theory has gained wide acceptance. If his theory is true, our brain has three layers, each of which receives music differently. The first, the reptilian brain, responds to music as vibration, sorting as it goes. The second, the limbic system, reacts to music emotionally, selecting appropriate emotive responses for different pieces of music. The third, the neocortex, responds to music intellectually, analyzing music and placing it into a context that we understand. We sort sounds in the brain stem, feel the emotion of those sounds in the limbic system, and translate those sounds into music in the cerebral cortex. Without this three-brain partnership, we could never create music. With it, the human world sings.

By itself, this information would make the case for the training beat of music, but it presents an incomplete picture. In the next chapter, "Left Right Left," we will turn our attention to a different view of our brains, focusing more fully on the neocortex.

Notes

1. Jourdain, R. (1997). *Music, The Brain, and Ecstasy: how music captures our imagination*. New York: Avon Books.

2. Ornstein, R., and Sobel, D. S. (1987). *The Healing Brain: breakthrough discoveries about how the brain keeps us healthy*. New York: Simon and Schuster.

3. MacLean, P. (1990). *The Triune Brain in Evolution*. New York: Plenum.

4. Hart, L. (1983). *The Human Brain and Human Learning*. New York: Longman.

5. Ormrod, J. (1995). *Human Learning,* 2nd ed. Englewood Cliffs, New Jersey: Merrill.

6. Campbell, D. (1997). *The Mozart Effect: tapping the power of music to heal the body, strengthen the mind, and unlock the creative spirit*. New York: Avon Books.

7. Jourdain, R. (1997).

8. Stevens, W., quoted in *Webster's Dictionary of Quotations*. (1995). New York: Smithmark Publishers.

9. Liszt, quoted in Grout, D., and Palisca, C. (1996). *A History of Western Music,* 5th ed. New York: W.W. Norton & Company.

10. Sylwester, R. A. (1995). *A Celebration of Neurons: an educator's guide to the human brain*. Alexandria, Virginia: Association for Supervision and Curriculum Development.

11. Mishkin, M. and Appenzeller, M. "The Anatomy of Memory." *Scientific American* (February 1987).

12. Lawlor, M., and Handley, P. (1996). *The Creative Trainer.* Cambridge, U.K.: University Press.

13. McGaugh, quoted by Rose, C., and Nicholl, M. (1997). *Accelerated Learning for the 21st Century: the six step plan to unlocking your master-mind*. New York: Delacorte Press.

14. Combarie, J., quoted in *Webster's Dictionary of Quotations*. (1995).

15. Ayto, J. (1990). *Dictionary of World Origins*. New York: Arcade Publishing.

16. Van Essen, D. "Letters." *Nature,* 385/6614 (January 23, 1997): 313–18.

Chapter 4

LEFT RIGHT LEFT

Next, we turn our attention to the Nobel Prize–winning work of psychobiologist Dr. Roger Sperry. Dr. Sperry and his team at the California Institute of Technology studied the effects of cutting the connecting tissue, the corpus callosum, between the two hemispheres of the brain. The team discovered that neither side of the brain knew what the other side was doing without the connecting tissue. In addition, and more important for our purposes, they discovered that each hemisphere generally has different functions and processes. As Dr. Sperry explained, "There appear to be two modes of thinking, verbal and nonverbal, represented separately in left and right hemispheres."[1] It is important to state that no one function is totally isolated in any one hemisphere. It is not a fact that one side does all of this or that. Rather, the findings relate to general tendencies that vary from person to person while remaining a fairly reliable predictor of human learning.[2]

The Human Brain—Top View

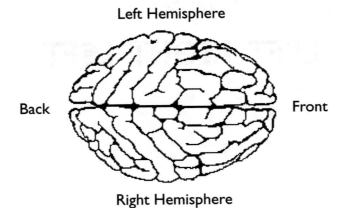

Left Hemisphere

Back ———————————————— Front

Right Hemisphere

Left Hemisphere

The left hemisphere is predominately logical and analytical. It processes ideas sequentially, in a linear fashion.[3] It tends to be the more academic brain, handling language,[4] math, and logic. The left hemisphere is about 90 percent better than the right hemisphere at recognizing words and about 70 percent better at identifying meaningless syllables or backward speech.[5]

Right Hemisphere

Whereas the left hemisphere tends to think sequentially, the right hemisphere thinks holistically, in concepts and metaphors. It needs to see the big picture first, perceiving, then absorbing, and then processing data, jumping from one idea to the next in no seeming order.[6] It is the creative side, dabbling in art, color, pictures, and music.[7]

A right-brained way to look at the problem is through drawing. The figure below graphically demonstrates the difference between the two modes of thinking. The left side of our figure is organized, rational, and earthbound, whereas the right side is free flowing, relaxed, and other worldly.

The interaction of these two hemispheres is fascinating. For example, if your right brain were sedated, you could describe an automobile, but not draw it. If the situation were reversed and your left brain were sedated, you could probably draw a car, but you would be unable to give it a name. We all use both sides of our brain, but most of us have a preference for one side or the other. If you would like to discover your own hemispheric preference, think about your desk. Is it neat and orderly or a mess? If every item is in its correct place, you may have left hemisphere tendencies. A sloppy and chaotic desktop may indicate right hemisphere dominance. For a more detailed self-assessment, see the table below.

Left-Right Brain Differences

Here is a resource for discovering your left-right preferences. Read the descriptive words below, and circle those that are most like you. The resulting list may give you an idea of your tendencies.

Left Dominance	Right Dominance
Structured	Spontaneous
Factual	Cerebral
Controlled	Emotional
Sequential	Metaphorical
Details	Possibilities
Measures	Connects
Comparing differences	Seeking Relationships
Rational	Empathic
Organized	Disorganized
Controlled	Relaxed
Objective	Subjective
Planned	Spontaneous
Analytical	Synthesizing
Prefers certain information	Plays hunches
Theoretical	Experimental
Sees cause and effect	Intuitive
Detailed	Patterned
What is . . .	What if . . .
Total:	Total:

Source: Miller, M. (1997). *Brain Styles: change your life without changing who you are.* New York: Simon and Schuster.

One costly effect of modern society is the predominance of the left hemisphere. Adults and businesses have spent centuries trying to be serious. This left emphasis permeates every facet of our lives. Stocks, ledgers, money, computers, machinery, and language all demand a heavy reliance on the left hemisphere. Too often, training has relied on reading, analysis, and lecture, while ignoring the learning relevance of right-hemispheric activities. Dr. Sperry elaborates: "One of the most important outcomes of the cerebral literality research is the increased insight and appreciation, in education and elsewhere, for the importance of nonverbal forms and components of learning, intellect, and communication."[8]

Jane Healy, in *Endangered Minds: Why Children Don't Think and What We Can Do about It,* extends the argument: "The trick in a well-functioning brain is to mix and match the abilities of the two hemispheres so that the most adaptive processing style is brought to bear on any learning situation."[9]

Music provides an ideal combination; it appeals to both hemispheres. Music is ordered sequentially for the left hemisphere, with rhythm and lyrics, and ordered simultaneously for the right hemisphere, with continuously evolving relationships and situations, including the performance of different instruments, sounds, and dynamics, harmonies over time, and melodies.

Music Note 6

Music appeals to both the left and right hemispheres:
♪ The left hemisphere processes rhythm and lyrics.
♪ The right hemisphere listens for melodies and harmonic relationships across time.

For example, if you heard a song while your left brain was sedated, you might not be able to speak, but you could still sing. If your right brain were sedated, you would probably be able to say the lyrics, but you might not find your voice to sing them. In other words, without a left brain, a person could sing for us, but could not explain the song. Without a right brain, the same person could explain their song to us, but could not perform it.[10]

In one study, nonmusician adults listened to familiar tunes at random, without either the melodies or rhythms. The rhythm alone did not provide enough information for recalling the music. Melody alone worked better than rhythm, but when both melody and rhythm were together, the recall was most effective.[11]

Finally, studies have discovered that the corpus callosum is generally **thicker** in musicians than in nonmusicians. Nonmusicians process melody in the right hemisphere, whereas musicians use the left hemisphere. Musicians may be processing melodies in a more analytic, "language-like" manner than nonmusicians.[12] This information is especially relevant for young people, and the importance of providing young people with a musical education. As a child becomes more musically studied, an interesting phenomenon occurs. Communication between the two hemispheres increases.[13] The right hemisphere processing ability develops in the left hemisphere. "Professional" music involves **both** hemispheres.[14] Children who study music establish brain connections that help them become more effective adult learners.

Music Note 7

Children who study music become effective adult learners.

A final word of caution is appropriate. Dominance is not absolute. Any time you discuss brain functions, you are shadow boxing. The generalizations are only useful to help us comprehend general tendencies. Anyone who tells you they know how the brain functions is fooling you, and themselves. We can, however, draw one unmistakable conclusion from what we know: music is an effective tool for engaging your learners' left and right hemispheres.

Notes

1. Sperry, R. (1973). "Lateral Specialization of Cerebral Function in the Surgically Separated Hemispheres." *The Psychophysiology of Thinking.* McGuigan, F., and Schoonover, R., eds. New York: Academic Press.

2. Polk, M., and Kertesz, A. "Music and Language in Degenerative Disease of the Brain." *Brain and Cognition,* 22/1 (1993): 98–117.

3. Bogen, J. E. "Some Educational Aspects of Hemispheric Specialization." *USCA Educator,* 17 (1975): 24–32.

4. Polk, M., and Kertesz, A. (1993).

5. Jourdain, R. (1997). *Music, The Brain, and Ecstasy: how music captures our imagination*. New York: Avon Books.

6. Bogen, J. E. (1975).

7. Polk, M., and Kertesz, A. (1993).

8. Sperry, R., quoted by Benson, F., and Zaidel, E. *The Dual Brain*. (1995). New York: The Guilford Press.

9. Healy, J. (1990). *Endangered Minds: why children don't think and what we can do about it*. New York: Simon and Schuster.

10. Young, R., and Nettelbeck, T. "The Abilities of a Musical Savant and His Family." *Journal of Autism and Development Disorders,* 25/3 (1995): 231–48.

11. Hébert, S., and Peretz, I. "Recognition of Music in Long-Term Memory: are melodic and temporal patterns equal partners?" *Memory & Cognition,* 25 (1997): 518–33.

12. Bever, T., and Chiarello, R. "Cerebral Dominance in Musicians and Non-musicians." *Science,* 185 (1974): 537–39.

13. Schlaug, G., Jancke, L., Haung, Y., Staiger, J., and Steinmetz, H. "Increased Corpus Callosum Size in Musicians." *Neuropsychologia,* 33/8 (1995): 1047–55.

14. Cohen, D., and Granot, R. (1992). *Cognitive Meanings of Musical Elements as Disclosed by ERP and Verbal Experiments*. Paper presented at the Second International Conference on Music Perception and Cognition, Los Angeles, California.

Chapter 5

BRAIN VIBRATIONS

Another view of brain functioning can be gained from understanding brain wave frequencies. The invention of the electroencephalograph machine (EEG) has allowed us to map the movement of electrical impulses within the brain, isolating these waves into four broad categories:

- Delta
- Theta
- Alpha
- Beta

Delta Waves

Delta waves (around 1 to 4 cycles) occur when you are in a deep, dreamless sleep. In this state, your brain, although not asleep, is at rest. As you begin to wake, your mind switches to Theta waves.

Brain Vibrations

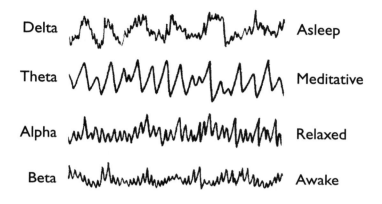

Delta		Asleep
Theta		Meditative
Alpha		Relaxed
Beta		Awake

Illustration by J. Chuck Johnson

Theta Waves

Theta waves (around 4 to 8 cycles per second) reflect your brains activities in the shallow stages of sleep, or in deep contemplation, or meditation. Your brain, in Theta state, exhibits free-flowing creativity, helping you experience sudden insights and inspirations.

Alpha Waves

Alpha waves (around 8 to 13 cycles per second) occur when your brain is in a nonaroused, relaxed state of awareness. Some of the most important Alpha moments of the day occur after you wake up, but before you focus your mind on the day's activities. In these moments, your mind is alert but relaxed, allowing your right hemisphere to engage in its free-flowing metaphorical visions without left hemisphere interference. You are also in Alpha when you read, study, or think deep thoughts.

Beta Waves

Beta waves (around 13 to 30 cycles per second) are the patterns of an awake, conscious mind, with the left hemisphere tending to dominate. This is the wave pattern you experience as you go about the daily business of living—talking, paying bills, doing work, analyzing situations, and concentrating on tasks at hand.[1]

Brain Waves and Music

All four waves are present in the brain at any given time, but EEG studies have confirmed that the amount of each varies as a person's brain becomes more alert or relaxed.[2] The higher the wave cycle, the more alert your brain becomes. During a normal day, our brains shift between Beta and Alpha states, depending on the circumstances that surround us. Fully functioning activities pull us into a Beta state, while an Alpha state is best for alert reflecting. (A truly boring training session will most likely shift your trainees into Theta state, as they start to fall asleep. If your trainees reach Delta state, their snoring will end your session.)

Fortunately, brains respond to music. Appropriately placed music can move your learners' minds from alert focus to reflective contemplation and back as often as your teaching activities require.

Slow, minor-key music encourages an Alpha state, so that your brain can relax and drop its left-hemispheric rationality. As your brain waves slow, the limbic system emotional centers grow dominant, allowing information to reach your subconscious and pass into your long-term memory. These brain wave patterns are especially useful for reviewing material and for creative visioning exercises.

One such opportunity may occur immediately after lunch. As the trainees' metabolisms slow down to absorb the recently consumed food, they start yawning. It looks like they are falling asleep. Most instructors attempt to wake everyone up with aggressive activity. In the process, they miss an incredible learning opportunity. Their trainees' bodies may be displaying tiredness, but their minds are actually in an alert Alpha state. This moment is ideal for review through reflection.

If a more active climate is required, faster, major-key music will wake a body up, encouraging it to become more active. Learners who are drifting into Alpha or Theta states will find their minds brought back to attention by up-tempo music.

Music Note 8

| ♪ Alpha brain waves encourage reflection. Use slow, minor-key music to foster Alpha waves. |
| ♪ Beta brain waves wake the brain up, making it more alert. Use fast, major-key music to encourage Beta waves. |

Next, we will add to our understanding of music's relationship to our minds, as, in "Musical Intelligence," we explore the effect music has on intelligence.

Notes

1. Rose, C., and Nicholl, M. J. (1997). *Accelerated Learning for the 21st Century: the six step plan to unlock your master-mind.* New York: Delacorte Press.

2. Herrmann, N. (1996). *The Whole Brain Business Book.* New York: McGraw-Hill.

Chapter 6

MUSICAL INTELLIGENCE

I've Got Rhythm

"Ms. King, can you come to the school for a visit?" the teacher's voice, distant and tinny, asked over the telephone. "We need to talk about Howard."

"Now what?" Tracy thought. "How could one seven year old get into so much trouble?" She did all she could. Working full-time and raising a child were difficult enough. But Howard was not your typical seven year old. It was not until first grade that the troubles began. The kid had no interest in anything. He constantly whined about how boring it all was. And the racket; the house was unbearable sometimes because of all the noise he made. The school had held him back last year, but she never understood it. "How does someone fail first grade?" she thought.

"Here we are, at two months into first grade (again!), and trouble is starting (again!)." Maybe a father figure would help, but there was not much that could be done about that. Howard's father had long since abandoned them.

When Tracy arrived at the school, she was ushered into the office immediately.

"Ms. King," said the teacher, "Thank you for coming in today. I wanted to talk about Howard."

"Why, what's he done wrong?" Tracy asked, expecting the worst.

"Nothing. In fact, it's just the opposite. We may have discovered something about Howard."

"Really?" This was not what she had expected. "What is that?"

"Well, he seems to have some musical ability."

"How's that?"

"Whenever I use music in the classroom, to learn the alphabet, for example, Howard comes alive. He taps his pencils, toes, hands, and anything else he can get a hold on. Do you see any signs of this activity at home?"

"Howard is always banging on something. It gets pretty annoying."

"Have you ever considered giving him drum lessons?"

"Not really. Money is tight and . . ."

"All he has to do is join the school's marching band. They need drummers anyway, and lessons come with joining. It may help him learn."

"Help him learn?" Tracy thought, "That's a strange idea." Out loud, she asked, "What's he going to do, beat out his school work?" She was immediately sorry. Her voice sounded more sarcastic than she had intended.

The teacher, if he noticed, did not react. "Well, not exactly. Remember last year, Howard was restless and disconnected? Nothing interested him."

Tracy remembered that all too well. If Howard was anything, it was restless and disconnected.

"We may have found a way to capture his attention. Some experts believe that traditional measures of intelligence don't tell the whole story, and that different people can be intelligent in different ways. According to their theory, Howard could actually be 'musically smart.' Joining the marching band may give him a reason to come to school. And, it gives us a second advantage. It may provide us with leverage to help him learn."

"Help him learn? How?" Tracy was getting intrigued. "Maybe this wasn't so crazy," she thought.

"Well, has he ever singsonged, or rapped, anything to learn it?"

"Yes. I used to 'rap' our address and phone number to him."

"It worked, didn't it?"

She began to understand. "Yes, it did."

"That's a strong clue. Encourage him to 'rap' his homework. If Howard has some musical intelligence, we should use it."

Tracy now realized that some of what she had identified as restlessness was actually natural ability surfacing. And the noise; it had a purpose too. She left the school promising three things. To the teacher she promised that she would discuss the band and "rap" homework with Howard. To herself, she promised to lighten up on her son. If what they suspected was true, she had a job to do. She needed to help Howard develop his "musical smarts."

Are people smarter because of music? Can the ability to hear music be considered an intelligence? As we saw during our discussion of the left and right hemispheres and of the corpus callosum growth in musicians, it would appear so. Howard Gardner and Daniel Goleman are two scholars who have spent years defining intelligence. In the process, their work has opened new possibilities for music's relationship to learning.

Multiple Intelligences

First, we will overview the works of Howard Gardner. Gardner theorized that humans have seven (now eight), and possibly more intelligences:

- bodily/kinesthetic
- interpersonal
- intrapersonal
- linguistic

- logical/mathematical
- naturalist
- visual/spatial
- musical/rhythmic[1]

Music Note 9

> *Music is a core learning intelligence.*

Multiple Intelligences Overview

Intelligence	Abilities
Bodily/Kinesthetic	Acting, participating in athletics, reading body language, dancing, exercising, using hand-eye coordination, handling objects, jumping, manipulating sensitive machinery
Interpersonal	Teaching others, leading groups, maintaining friendships, sensing moods, respecting rights, empathizing, leading groups, connecting with others, resolving conflicts
Intrapersonal	Being self-aware, evaluating, self-directing, controlling impulses, comprehending self, developing differentiated opinions, self-motivating
Logical/Mathematical	Analyzing, computing, deducing, estimating, experimenting, problem solving, reasoning, applying logic, working with numbers
Musical/Rhythmic	Appreciating and recognizing music, composing, keeping time, performing, recognizing rhythm, singing
Naturalist	Caring for animals and plants, predicting the weather, protecting the environment, recognizing species
Verbal/Linguistic	Communicating, debating, discussing, understanding languages, listening, reading, speaking, spelling, writing
Visual/Spatial	Designing architecture and graphics, coordinating color, decorating, painting, reading maps, sculpting, drawing, visualizing

SOURCES: Gardner, H. (1991). *The Unschooled Mind: how children think and how schools should teach.* New York: Basic Books

Kagan, S., and Kagan M. (1998). *Multiple Intelligences: the complete MI book.* San Clemente, California: Kagan Cooperative Learning.

In his book *Multiple Intelligences,* Gardner describes his theory as a "pluralistic view of the mind, recognizing many different and discrete facets of cognition, acknowledging that people have different cognitive strengths and contrasting cognitive styles."[2] His approach emphasizes the ability to survive and lead a productive and fulfilling life within a cultural framework through a reliance on innate strengths.

Gardner's theory features two ideas important to the teaching power of music:

- A person's core intelligences need to be engaged in learning.
- People need to learn in multiple ways.

A person's core intelligences need to be engaged in learning. Gardner believes that even though all intelligences are present to some degree within every individual, some individuals show innate abilities in specific intelligences. "Not all people have the same interests and abilities: not all of us learn in the same way."[3] For many people, the lack of variety in learning methods made school a frustrating experience. Learning that matches and mirrors a person's intelligence helps that person feel more engaged and competent. It also enriches the learning experience, making it more fulfilling.

People need to learn in multiple ways. Gardner assumes that people need to be engaged at many different levels to learn. "These intelligences constitute cognitive resources by virtue of which an individual may effect a meaningful connection to a content area."[4]

He recommends using at least five approaches from *Multiple Intelligences* to reach your learners, giving them a multidimensional view of the learning topic. In Gardner's approach, one subject might be taught in a multitude of ways. For instance, a World War II lesson could be taught as follows:

- **Bodily/Kinesthetic**—Marching like soldiers
- **Interpersonal**—Small group discussion about the effects of the war
- **Intrapersonal**—Individual reflection on the meaning of war

- **Linguistic**—Verbal remembrances from veterans
- **Logical/Mathematical**—Statistics demonstrating the high cost of the war
- **Naturalist**—War's effect on the environment
- **Visual/Spatial**—Drawings and maps of battlefields
- **Musical/Rhythmic**—Music from the war period

This multiple approach exposes learners to a wide range of learnings. In the process of engaging the learner at their individual intelligences level, the learner is encouraged to participate fully in all learning activities, furthering the development of intelligences that are not a strength.

Unfortunately, a multilevel approach is not the norm. Gardner states that individuals are the victims of this "single-minded" approach to education, in which a learner only is exposed to the learning methods preferred by the teacher, not the learner. "It is clear that many talents, if not intelligences, are overlooked nowadays; individuals with these talents are the chief casualities of the single-minded, single funneled approach to the mind."[5] Most of the research around Multiple Intelligences, and Gardner's own focus, is child education, but the same logic applies to adults. If the material being trained speaks to the adult learner's core intelligences, that learner will be more inclined to feel valued and, as a result, will participate more fully. Music is one more tool for breaking through a learner's wall of resistance.

Emotional Intelligence

We have long known that music touches our emotions. Beethoven described music as "the mediator between the life of the senses and the life of the spirit."[6] Aldois Huxley believed that "after silence, that which comes nearest to expressing the inexpressible is music."[7] Paul MacLean's work, identifying the emotional functions of the limbic system, made the connection between music and emotion understandable. But it is Daniel Goleman's work that establishes the importance of emotion in everyday life and suggests that music is relevant to success.

Goleman focused on the limbic system and the importance of emotive skills in life. He called his theory "Emotional Intelligence." The main tenet of Emotional Intelligence is that, as the human brain developed and people became more intellectual, they forgot the emotional voice within. Goleman believes that people need the emotive limbic system skills; that being in touch with your own emotions, and those of others, leads to success; and that the more successful a person becomes, the less expertise matters, and the more emotional skills become critical. Goleman describes emotions as background murmur that we ignore until it surfaces in a moment of emotionalism. He recommends that we develop our ability to understand our emotions and give voice to the usually inexpressible feelings within.[8]

Music is a window to those emotions. In the words of Heinz Kohut, it serves "as an extra verbal mode of mental functioning, permits a specific, subtle regression to pre-verbal, i.e., to truly primitive forms of mental experience."[9]

This regression appears to occur regardless of human differences. People of all ages, genders, and cultural backgrounds experience the same emotions when listening to like selections of music.[10] Music produces, within the limbic system, a feeling of liking or disliking, and a level of excitement or arousal. When both liking or disliking and excitement or arousal are present, specific emotions are created.[11] Therefore, music can help people touch their emotions, allowing them to communicate more deeply.

John Blacking, in his *Commonsense View of All Music*, opined, "The development of the senses and the education of the emotions through the arts are not merely desirable options. They are essential both for balanced action and the effective use of the intellect."[12] "Learning which involves the whole person of the learner, feelings as well as intellect," believes Carl Rogers, "is the most lasting and pervasive."[13]

Goleman expands this theme. He believes learning would be more effective if it focused on emotional intelligence in addition to traditional learning. Music, used emotionally, can reach to the core emotion of a subject, allowing for a deeper connection. For example:

- Communication skills training can be tied into the emotional effect of improperly delivered messages through a song about friendship lost because of miscommunication.

- Motivational skills can be encouraged with music. A number of championship and celebration songs exist that can re-create the emotional side effects of achievement and that can inspire motivation.

Trainers, armed with this information, can use music to communicate with learners at a deeper level of understanding, touching their emotional intelligence.

Music Note 10

Music reaches people's intelligence:
♪ helping people feel engaged and competent
♪ providing a multidimensional view of learning topics
♪ breaking through a trainee's wall of resistance
♪ touching people's emotions, reaching a deeper level of understanding and communication

Both the Multiple Intelligences and the Emotional Intelligence theories add to our comprehension of the training beat. Next, we will explore ways people have used music to learn.

Notes

1. Gardner, H. (1983). *Frames of Mind*. New York: Basic Books.

2. Gardner, H. (1993). *Multiple Intelligences: the theory in practice*. New York: Basic Books.

3. Gardner, H. (1983).

4. Gardner, H., and Krechevsky, M. (1993). "The Emergence and Nurturance of Multiple Intelligences in Early Childhood: the project spectrum approach." *Multiple Intelligences: the theory in practice*. New York: Basic Books.

5. Gardner, H., and Walters, J. (1993). "A Rounded Vision." *Multiple Intelligences: the theory in practice*. New York: Basic Books.

6. Beethoven, L., quoted by Burton, S. (1984). *The Home Book of Quotations: classical and modern*. New York: Greenwich House.

7. Huxley, A., quoted in *Webster's Dictionary of Quotations*. (1995). New York: Smithmark Publishers.

8. Goleman, D. (1995). *Emotional Intelligence: why it can matter more than IQ*. New York: Bantam Books.

9. Kohut, H. "Some Psychological Effects of Music and Their Relation to Music Therapy." *Music Therapy*, 5 (1995): 17–20.

10. Brown, J. D., and Mankowski, T. A. "Self-Esteem, Mood, and Self-Evaluation: changes in mood and the way you see you." *Journal of Personality and Social Psychology*, 64/3 (1993): 421–30; Robazza, C., Macaluso, C., and D'Urso, V. "Emotional Reactions to Music by Gender, Age, and Expertise." *Perceptual and Motor Skills*, 79/2 (1994): 939–44.

11. North, A. C., and Hargreaves, D. J. "Liking, Arousal Potential, and the Emotions Expressed by Music." *Scandinavian Journal of Psychiatry*, 38 (1997): 45–53.

12. Blacking, J. (1987). *A Commonsense View of All Music*. Cambridge: Cambridge University Press.

13. Rogers, C. (1969). *Freedom to Learn*. Columbus, Ohio: Merrill.

Chapter 7

MUSIC AND LEARNING

The Wall

"Tear down this wall." And so it began. Well, actually, the end began. That monstrosity had stood, defiled and defaced, for almost thirty years. From the day it was built, we fought against it. The cost was enormous; at least five hundred people died in escape attempts. (The butchers painted it white so that escapees would make better targets at night!) No more lives could be lost.

In the few short months since the U.S. President Ronald Reagan stood at the Brandenburg Gate with West German Chancellor Helmut Kohl and shouted "Mr. Gorbachev, tear down this wall," events had accelerated. Soviet General Secretary Mikhail Gorbachev, during a trip to the Eastern state, bluntly informed the dictators that Soviet troops would *not keep them in power. The people with behind-the-scenes power, the Americans and the Russians, always suspicious, now amazingly agreed.*

We began the final push with public silence. Husbands, wives, grand-mothers, grandfathers, children—all walking, all protesting, all in silence. (We could not afford to antagonize the East German security police, the Stasi. Any mistakes by us would cost lives.)

The pressure of our silence led to easing of restrictions. That, in turn, led to more pressure. Once the Hungarians opened their borders, alter-nate escape routes were possible. Events accelerated when, in a press conference, an East German official, bowing to reality, casually men-tioned that the state would lift restrictions on travel between the two halves of our country. The word spread like lightning across the West. Our television signals, picked up in the East, spread the news. Suddenly, the wall was irrelevant, a white elephant in our midst.

So, there we stood at the wall, for days, waiting. It began slowly, from the east side of the wall; one phrase, repeated, becoming a chant: "We are the people." The chant inspired those of us on the west side, and we joined in. The Stasi, as if hearing the collective conscious of their country, did nothing. That chant became our rallying call. Soon, "We are the people" became "We are one people." The chant grew. It became song. We sang, shouted, danced, and celebrated, as to the beat of our song, and in time with our countrymen on both sides, we tore down the Berlin Wall.[1]

People have been teaching with music for centuries. Our ancient ancestors, before written language, in hostile environments with short life expectancies, needed to communicate survival information from generation to generation. Music most likely filled that need. Primitive societies the world over still exhibit remnants of these survival tech-niques:

- "All unpolished peoples sing and act; they sing about what they do and thus sing histories. Their songs are the archives of their people, the treasury of their science and religion."[2]

- In Australia, Aborigine music is multilayered—a life's study that only the most devoted of the population reaches. The information an Aborigine needs to be able to completely understand the meanings of his world are all there, requiring the individual to learn customs, history, and social order through the music. "Learning music is a means of entering the highest reaches of his culture's intellectual and spiritual development."[3]

- Professional musicians (griots) act as historians in many African societies.[4] "The African sings about work, about hunting, about money, about women, about canoeing, about planting—in short about all things that men dwell naturally upon in their minds."[5]

- The African Tiv tribe uses music to teach and define cultural norms within its society.[6]

- The Kaluli tribe in Papua New Guinea uses songs to help map important geographic locations.[7]

- Among the Mande peoples of the west African savanna, professional bards still recount the histories of powerful lineages and offer counsel to contemporary rulers.[8]

This reliance on music is common in preindustrial societies. As assembly lines replaced craftsmen and agriculture, people focused more on the left-hemispheric skills required for industrialization. Music and emotion became background murmur to production, mathematics, and finance.

People today have largely forgotten the reliance of our ancestors on music, even though remnants of this usage still exist:

- Religious groups rely on hymns and poems to pass their traditions and beliefs from generation to generation.[9]

- From the "Star Spangled Banner" to "God Save the Queen" to the "Michigan Fight Song," virtually every country, school, and association has a theme song.

- Even the armed forces get into the musical spirit. The United States Army sings "The Caissons Go Rolling Along," the Navy "Anchors Aweigh," and the Marines "From the Halls of Montezuma."

These songs remind the listeners of long-held traditions and important historical events, motivate and inspire group solidarity, and define group norms to newer members.

In my seminars on the teaching power of music, I often ask the question "How has music helped you learn?" Invariably, a participant responds that music helped them as a child learn their alphabet, words, or math. Children have no preconceived notions of how they should behave, or how to learn. Yet they successfully grow, learn, and become functioning adults. They often learn by singing. Nursery rhymes, children's tunes, and chants teem with life lessons. "In 1642, Columbus sailed the ocean blue," "*I* before *E* except after *C*" are but two examples of childhood learning in rhythm. Popular children's television, such as *Sesame Street, Mr. Roger's Neighborhood,* and *Schoolhouse Rock,* effectively use music to teach necessary life skills to children. To explore the effectiveness of this technique, see the lyrical learning table below.

Lyrical Learning

Complete the musical phrases listed below.

The itsy bitsy spider went up the __ __ __ __ __ __ __ __ __ __.

Now I know my ABCs, tell me what you __ __ __ __ __ __ __ __ __.

Mary had a little lamb, its fleece was __ __ __ __ __ __ __ __ __ __ __.

Twinkle, twinkle, little star, how I wonder what __ __ __ __ __ __ __.

I've been working on the railroad, all the __ __ __ __ __ __ __ __ __ __ __.

As children mature, they become more "adult," shunning childish ways. Music and rhyme become silly, juvenile. Over time, the noise of daily life drowns out the music. People either forget these learning methods or become reluctant to use them. Adulthood eventually wins, and the beat is lost. Except, of course, for new children. They know all too well the teaching power of music.

Music Note 11

| Children learn by singing. Adults should too.

Research has begun validating the theory that adults can learn with music.

An early pioneer of music and learning was the Bulgarian doctor and psychiatrist Georgi Lozanov. In the 1960s, Dr. Lozanov discovered that music could increase learning. He developed what he called "concerts," passive and active.

Dr. Lozanov used active concerts as a way of teaching language skills. He would select a dynamic piece of music (such as a Beethoven symphony) and recite language phrases in time with, and matching the dynamics of, the music. Through his experiments with active concerts, he found that this technique, although not often applied today, was effective. Perhaps the method is not widely used because of a "coolness" factor. It takes nerve to stand in front of a group of adults and talk dynamically along with a symphony.

Lozanov's second kind of concert he called "passive." In a passive concert, slower music is played. People are encouraged to enter a relaxed state of awareness, opening the mind to incoming information. This technique has a commonality with the MacLean and Goleman limbic system comments. Appropriate musical selections slow the brain waves down to Alpha state, about 8 and 12 cycles per second, creating a relaxing, peaceful state of mind. By tapping into the pleasant emotions of the limbic system, information passes into long-term memory. Lozanov found that people could learn language skills at least four times faster through a passive concert than they could in a traditional classroom environment.[10] These theories have been so embraced that a whole discipline, called accelerated learning, has been built around them.

Additional research, although not entirely conclusive, is validating music's usefulness as a teaching tool. The Music Learning News offers a sampling of these findings, including:

- increased development for fetuses[11]
- increased math skills for elementary school students[12]
- higher SAT verbal and math scores[13]
- higher admittance to medical school by music majors[14]

The research receiving the most attention, and controversy, is the work of cognitive development professor Frances Rauscher and her team. In a series of experiments, the team found that listening to Mozart's Piano Sonata K448 created a temporary intellectual boast that increased spatial scores of college students on IQ tests.[15] Dr. Rauscher's team concluded that "listening to music can affect this form of intelligence in adults (spatial-temporal abilities), although for only a very short period of time (10–15 minutes)."[16]

Dr. Rauscher also found that children who receive music training demonstrate increased spatial-temporal abilities: "We have found that music training, provided to young children, causes long-term enhancement of spatial-temporal abilities."[17]

To practicing musicians, these findings are no surprise. Musicians have long known that they are, well . . . different. Nonmusicians rarely understand their thought processes. Musicians are described as "flaky, odd, or weird." A musician's brain is wired differently than that of the average person. As we saw during our exploration of Roger Sperry's left-right hemisphere experiments, musicians, and people who had musical training when they were young, have a wider connecting bridge, the corpus callosum, between their left and right hemispheres. This does not make musicians any smarter. In fact, I know some incredibly stupid musicians. But it does allow musicians to use more of their whole brain.

The popular press has latched onto Rauscher's research, proclaiming that Mozart makes you smarter. Books, CDs, and even whole curricula have been built around this so-called effect. In one instance, Georgia Governor Zell Miller arranged for his state to purchase Mozart's music CDs for new mothers. Recording companies eventually paid $105,000 for the CDs and new mothers received them as they left Georgia's hospitals.[18]

Music Learning News

All the news your mind needs!

Ooh, Baby Baby

Dr. Thomas Verny, in *The Secret Life of the Unborn Child,* describes how western classical music, played at a rhythm of 60 beats per minute, equivalent to that of a resting human heart, provides an environment conducive to creative and intellectual development of the child.

Easy As ABC

Neurological Research reports that preschoolers who studied piano performed 34 per cent better in spatial and temporal reasoning ability than preschoolers who spent the same amount of time learning to use computers.

I Love Music

Students in two Rhode Island elementary schools given a sequential, skill-building music program showed a marked improvement in math skills according to Gardiner, Fox, Jeffrey, and Knowles.

Piano Kids

After eight months of keyboard lessons, Rauscher, Shaw, Levine, Ky and Wright discovered that preschoolers demonstrated a 46 percent boost in their spatial reasoning IQ.

Classical Gas

Rauscher and Shaw reported in Nature that listening to Mozart's Piano Sonata K448 significantly increased spatial scores of college students on IQ tests.

Imagine It

Music has been proven to enhance creativity by helping people imagine what they want to create, according to the Journal of Creative Behavior.

The Language Of Music

The Journal of Music Therapy reports that music is a useful tool for learning a second language to children in preschool.

Pump It Up

Miller and Schyb report that increasing the tempo of background music increases reading speed for students.

Music Takes Ya Higher

According to the College Entrance Examination Board, students who study music scored higher on both the verbal and math portions of the SAT than students who did not study music.

Run, Run, Run

Olympic Gold medal winner Michael Johnson reported that listening to jazz helped him prepare for the 400-meter race, and his record-breaking 19.32-second performance on the 200-yard dash can be partially attributed to rap.

Doctor Music

Phi Delta Kappan reports that 66 percent of music majors, who applied to medical school were admitted, the highest percentage of any group seeking admittance.

Music Learning News References in order of appearance top to bottom

1. Verny, T. (1981). *The Secret Life of the Unborn Child.* New York: Dell.

2. Rauscher, F., Shaw, G., Levine, L., Wright, E., Dennis, W., and Newcomb, R. "Music Improves Reasoning in Preschool Children," *Neurological Research,* 19 (February 1997): 121–27.

3. Gardiner, M. F., Fox, A., Jeffrey, D., and Knowles, F. "Learning Improved by Arts Training," *Nature,* 381/6580 (May 23, 1996): 284.

4. Rauscher, F., et al. (February 1997).

5. Rauscher, F., Shaw, G., and Ky, K. "Music and Spatial Task Performance," *Nature,* 365/6447 (1993): 611.

6. Adaman, J., and Blaney, P. "The Effects of Musical Mood Induction on Creativity," *Journal of Creative Behavior,* 29/2 (1995): 95–108.

7. Cartwright, J., and Huckaby, G. "Intensive Preschool Language Program," *Journal of Music Therapy,* 9/3 (1972): 147–55.

8. Miller, L., and Schyb, M. "Facilitation and Interference by Background Music," *Journal of Music Therapy,* 26/1 (1989): 42–54.

9. College Entrance Examination Board. "Music Is Key," *Music Educators Journal* (January 1996): 6.

10. Reported by Miles, E. (1997). *Tune Your Brain: using music to manage your mind, body, and mood.* New York: Berkeley Books.

11. Miller, A., and Coen, D. "The Case for Music in the Schools." *Phi Delta Kappan,* 75/6 (February 1994).

Governmental enthusiasm and corporate goodness aside, trainers should proceed with caution. The experimental results have been difficult to reproduce.[19] Harvard Medical School researcher Christopher Chabris claims to have largely disproven the whole notion. "The bottom-line message is that there is either no Mozart effect or a very small Mozart effect."[20] Notice what Dr. Rauscher says about her own work: "I find that 'Mozart makes you smarter' thing is quite a bit of a leap. This evidence is tentative at best. Listening to music has some effects, but they don't last, as far as we know so far."[21]

Additionally, Dr. Rauscher is very specific that other kinds of music may have the same effect as Mozart's. "Others have replicated the effect with Schubert's music. I think any music that is complex, regardless of the period, would have similar effects."[22]

Let the scientists argue over which music makes you smartest. The teaching power of music is not dependent on a blind allegiance to any composer, style, or piece of music. It lies instead in using tools that appeal to your participants' reptilian, limbic, and neocortex brains; engage their left and right hemispheres; honor their multiple and emotional intelligences; and pull forth Beta, Theta, and Alpha brain waves. Training has a beat when a musical teaching tool enhances learning. Music, applied in a commonsense fashion to the learning situation at hand, has true power.

Notes

1. "As It Happened: the Berlin Wall." (1999). The History Channel. New York.

2. Herder, J., quoted by Storr, A. (1992). *Music and the Mind*. New York: Random House, Inc.

3. Ellis, C. J. (1985). *Aboriginal Music: education for living*. St. Lucia, Australia: University of Queensland Press.

4. *The 1995 Grolier Multimedia Encyclopedia*. (1995). vr. 7.0.2. Grolier Electronic Publishing, Inc.

5. Hailey, L. (1957). *An African Survey*. New York: Oxford University Press.

6. Keil, C. (1979). *Tiv Song*. Chicago: University of Chicago Press.

7. Feld, S. (1990). *Sound and Sentiment: birds, weeping, poetics and song in Kaluli expression*. Philadelphia: University of Pennsylvania Press.

8. *The 1995 Grolier Multimedia Encyclopedia*. (1995).

9. Rowland, M. (1998). "Adult Learning through Religious Music in an African American Church." *DAI*, 59/08A (1998): 28.

10. Lozanov, G. (1978). *Suggestology and Outlines of Suggestopedy*. London: Gordon and Breach Science Publishers.

11. Verny, T. (1981). *The Secret Life of the Unborn Child*. New York: Dell.

12. Gardiner, M., Fox, A., Jeffrey, D., and Knowles, F. "Learning Improved by Arts Training." *Nature*, 381/6580 (May 23, 1996): 284.

13. College Entrance Examination Board. "Music Is Key." *Music Educators Journal* (January 1996): 6.

14. Miller, A., and Coen, D. "The Case for Music in the Schools." *Phi Delta Kappan*, 75/6 (February 1994).

15. Rauscher, F., Shaw, G., and Ky, K. "Music and Spatial Task Performance." *Nature*, 365/6447 (1993): 611.

16. Rauscher, F. (1997). "Music Training and Spatial-Temporal Reasoning." ARTSEDGE Virtual Conference, <www.artsedge.kennedy-center.org>.

17. Ibid.

18. Viadero, D. "Music on the Mind." *Education Week on the Web* (April 8, 1998). <www.edweek.org>.

19. Steele, K., dalla Bella, S., Peretz, I., Dunlop, T., Dawe, L., and Humphrey, G. "Prelude or Requiem for the Mozart Effect?" *Nature*, 400/6747 (1999): 827–28.

20. Chabris, C., quoted in the *Orlando Sentinel*, Orlando, Florida, August 27, 1999.

21. Rauscher, F., quoted by Debra Viadero in "Music on the Mind." *Education Week on the Web* (April 8, 1998). <www.edweek.org>.

22. Rauscher, F. "Online Chat with Dr. Rauscher." ARTSEDGE Virtual Conference. (February 6, 1998): 7:00–8:00 P.M. <www.artsedge.kennedy-center.org>.

Part Two

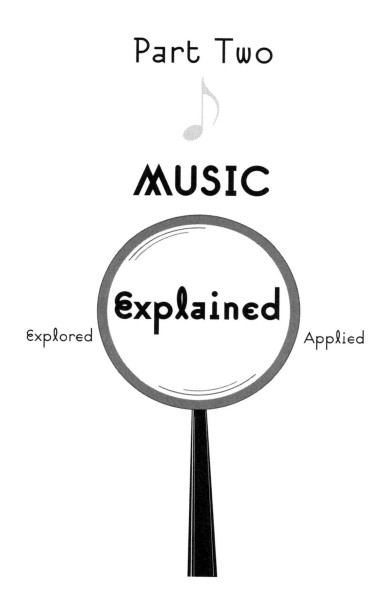

MUSIC

Explored   Explained   Applied

Music is nothing else but wild sounds
civilized into time and tune.

—Thomas Fuller

Chapter 8
THE MUSICAL PULSE

The Arrival

"It has arrived!" shouted the housekeeper, waking him with a shake. This was not the way he planned it. Years ago, he would have heard the knock at the door, but not now. The best he could manage was a nod of understanding. He dragged himself out of his feathered bed. He was exhausted but would gladly awake for this.

Months ago, when his brother, Caspar Carl, told the craftsman what was required, the craftsman argued against it. "Double the strings?" he whined in disbelief, "Mein Herr, it is not easily done. The soundboard, how could it handle the tension? And think of the noise. A piano at twice the volume! Who would want such an instrument?"

"The master would," replied Casper Carl, "You know how demanding he is. Let him worry about the volume. Build him his instrument." With that, the contract had been drawn, and the piano built. Now, finally, it was here.

He threw on his clothing and rushed to the parlor. The proud craftsman tried to demonstrate the piano's features for him. He brushed past and rushed out of the house. "The asses," he thought. "They must not know. Let them think I am temperamental. Imagine what would happen if my patrons discovered this secret; a great composer whose ears will not work."

He walked the woods with drooping eyelids. His eyes, always small, were bare slits. Cursed, he was tired. He had worked all night on a passage for the new composition. Often when he wrote, he would scribble any old song between major themes. Later, he would remove those stolen phrases and replace them with the new material. Last night had been one such occasion. He could imagine the work in his head. He knew how it would sound. With this piano, he might once again hear the notes.

By the time one circuit of the woods was over, they had gone. He reentered the house and rushed to the parlor. There it was. It was magnificent! The soundboard reinforcement was almost invisible. But what did it matter anyway, as long as he could hear the instrument. The master sat at the piano bench, placed his left ear on the piano cover. Slowly, carefully, hesitantly he began to play. Oh, the joy. He could feel the vibrating pulse. He could hear some sound. The great Beethoven could touch his music again.

Anyone, given a rudimentary understanding of music, can train with a beat. We will now overview the important music theory principles. This chapter may be too basic for musicians reading *Training with a Beat: The Teaching Power of Music,* but it will provide nonmusicians with all the information required to intelligently harness the teaching power of music.

So, what is music, and what separates music from noise? The sounds of nature provide a useful starting point for defining music. Birds are said to "sing," but what they really do is repeat patterns. The relationship between these sounds has little variation, and hence little musical value. Birds do not control their song. They repeat patterns seared into bird memory. There are no bird sheet music, no bird CDs, no bird symphonies. Imagine an orchestra of birds performing a bird concerto written two hundred years ago by Birdhoven and you begin to see the difficulty. No such concerto is possible. Most sounds in nature in fact do not really make "music." They are too random and cannot be controlled. Natural sounds, although soothing, are not music. Only humans have the capability to organize sounds into music.

Composer Igor Stravinsky differentiated noise from music with this definition: "I conclude that tonal elements become music only by virtue of their being organized, and that such organization presupposes a conscious human act."[1]

Stravinsky has it right. It is not the sounds that make the music; it is the relationship between sounds that our ears hear as music. The *American Heritage Collegiate Dictionary* definition of music supports Stravinsky's position:

> Mu sic (myoo' zik) *n*. The art of arranging sounds in time so as to produce a continuous, unified, and evocative composition, as through melody, and rhythm.[2]

Music Note 12

Music is organized sound.

Humans arrange these sounds by deciding which sounds to use, what order these sounds should be heard in, and, most important for organization, how long each sound should be. The two primary elements involved in those decisions are rhythm and melody.

Music Note 13

> The two primary elements of music are rhythm and melody.

Rhythm and melody find their way into
the inward places of the soul.

—Plato[3]

Rhythm

First, let us turn our attention to the beat, for "to study rhythm is to study all of music. Rhythm both organizes, and is itself organized by, all the elements which create and shape musical processes."[4]

The beat is everywhere. Electricity pulses in a beat. Our microwave ovens, copy machines, windshield wipers, computers, and televisions beat in time. Rhythm is a natural phenomenon in humans. Our breath, pulse, heart rate, speech, and walking pace all beat in time. Our bodies pulse with electrical charges. We are beat driven. In the words of Gloria Estefan and Enrique E. Garcia, "You can fight it every day, but no matter what you say, the rhythm is gonna get'cha." *[5]

Our ancestors must have been in tune with their beat. The earliest musical instruments, probably drums, mimicked this beat of life as early people fell naturally into the rhythmic pulses familiar to them. Gradually, over time, Western music developed its rhythm around two physical activities, walking and swaying.

Somewhere around 1650, an effective system of codifying these beats, a time signature, was established.[6] Just as a clock is an agreed on representation of time, a time signature is an agreed on representation of rhythm. It is our method for documenting the accents that occur within a piece of music, so that a musical composition can be performed with the same rhythm each and every time.

A time signature is represented by a fraction. The upper number indicates the number of beats that occur within a time period, or measure, while the lower number indicates the type of note that receives a beat.

---

* "Rhythm Is Gonna Get You," written by Gloria Estefan and Enrique Garcia. Copyright 1987. Foreign Imported Productions & Publishing, Inc. (BMI) International Rights Secured. All Rights Reserved.

$$\text{Time Signature} = \frac{\text{Number of beats that occur within a time period}}{\text{Type of note that receives a beat}}$$

The number of beats in a measure is determined by the beat that receives the most emphasis. That beat is often considered to be the start of the measure. A repeating of the primary emphasis indicates a starting over—the beginning of a new measure.

Music Note 14

A time period signifies the number of beats per time period over the kind of note that receives a beat.

Western music relies primarily on two different time signatures, $\frac{4}{4}$ and $\frac{3}{4}$.

Music Note 15

The two primary time signatures are $\frac{4}{4}$ and $\frac{3}{4}$.

$\frac{4}{4}$ **time.** In classic $\frac{4}{4}$ time, the first and the fifth beats receive strong accents. The first beat indicates the start of the measure. The fifth beat indicates the beginning of a new measure. You can feel the $\frac{4}{4}$ pulse by emphasizing every fifth step you take as you walk.

It should also be noted that rock music turns the whole $\frac{4}{4}$ emphasis on its head. Instead of emphasizing every fifth beat, rock music accents every other beat, with the strongest accent occurring on the fourth beat. For trainers using music with either a classic or rock feel, the key consideration remains the same. On every fifth beat, the emphasis starts over.

$\frac{4}{4}$ time is the workhorse of modern music. Most of the music we listen to—rock, pop, classical, marches, and polkas—pulse in some derivative of $\frac{4}{4}$.

$\frac{3}{4}$ **time.** The other primary representation of meter is $\frac{3}{4}$ time. Because of rock and pop music, we listen to a lot less $\frac{3}{4}$ time. It is not as familiar to us, but most lilting pieces of music, waltzes and some ballads for instance, are in $\frac{3}{4}$ time.

In $\frac{3}{4}$ time, the first and the fourth beats receive strong accents. The first beat indicates the start of the measure, the fourth beat indicates the beginning of a new measure. You can feel the $\frac{3}{4}$ pulse when you sway side to side. Simply count to three on each sway. It is an ideal pulse for hoisting a stein of beer and singing.

Notation of $\frac{4}{4}$ and $\frac{3}{4}$. The length of time a sound is performed within a measure is documented through the use of a notation system, with whole, half, quarter, eighth, and sixteenth notes. In $\frac{4}{4}$ time:

- The whole note receives all four beats in a measure.
- The half note is half the length of a whole note and receives two beats.
- The quarter note is one quarter the length of a whole note and receives one beat.
- The eighth note is one eighth the length of a whole note and receives one half of a beat.
- The sixteenth note is one sixteenth the length of a whole note and receives one fourth of a beat.

$\frac{4}{4}$ Time

The notation system for $\frac{3}{4}$ time is the same as that of $\frac{4}{4}$, but it is divided somewhat differently:

- In $\frac{3}{4}$ time, the whole note is usually not used. Instead, a dotted half note receives all three beats in a measure.

- The half note maintains the same value as it does in $\frac{4}{4}$, receiving two beats, but is two thirds the length of the whole note.

- The quarter note maintains the same value as it does in $\frac{4}{4}$, receiving one beat, but is one third the length of a whole note.

- The eighth note maintains the same value as it does in $\frac{4}{4}$, receiving one half of a beat, but is one sixth the length of a whole note.

- The sixteenth note maintains the same value as it does in $\frac{4}{4}$, receiving one fourth of a beat, but is one twelfth the length of a whole note.

$\frac{3}{4}$ Time

Some experts will argue that other time signatures are equally important. The more common of these other time signatures are listed below.

Other Time Signatures

Meter	Symbol	Pulse	Where the Beat Falls
Two-Two	$\frac{2}{2}$	Two beats to a measure	The half note receives the beat
Two-Four	$\frac{2}{4}$	Two beats to a measure	The quarter note receives the beat
Five-Four	$\frac{5}{4}$	Five beats to a measure	The quarter note receives the beat
Six-Eight	$\frac{6}{8}$	Six beats to a measure	Every seventh eighth note receives a beat

There are as many time signatures as there are numbers to create them. It is not important to know all the possibilities—$\frac{4}{4}$ and $\frac{3}{4}$ will suffice. The magic of these time signatures is in their familiarity. Your trainees are comfortable with them. Unusual time signatures that draw attention to themselves will interfere with the learning at hand. When selecting music for training, try to walk or sway to it. If it is difficult to do either, then the piece of music is in a less-common time signature. Do not use it. The beat of this selection may distract your trainees from the learning you desire.

Music Note 16

Select training music you can walk or sway to.

Next, we will turn our attention to the second half of the musical definition, sound.

Notes

1. Stravinsky, I. (1947). *Poetics of Music*. New York: Vintage Books.

2. *The American Heritage Collegiate Dictionary*, 3rd ed. (1997). Boston: Houghton Mifflin Company.

3. Plato, quoted by Ehrich, E., and De Bruhl, M. (1996). *The International Thesaurus of Quotations*. New York: HarperCollins Publishers, Inc.

4. Cooper, G., and Meyer, L. (1960). *The Rhythmic Structure of Music*. Chicago: University of Chicago Press.

5. Estefan, G., and Garcia, E. "Rhythm Is Gonna' Get You." Miami: Foreign Imported Productions. Used with permission. All rights reserved.

6. Grout, D., and Palisca, C. (1996). *A History of Western Music*, 5th ed. New York: W.W. Norton & Company.

Chapter 9

THE MUSICAL SOUND

Making Melodies

Vibrations. We have discovered that two elements are essential for the creation of music—rhythm and melody. We have defined rhythm and seen how tones are created and documented for future performance. Let us now turn our attention to creating melodies from sound.

Sound is a physical phenomenon. Air molecules, when exposed to vibrations, create what our ears hear as sound.

Music Note 17

Air molecules plus vibrations create sound.

It is easy to create vibrations of your own. If you were to take a crystal wine glass, fill it halfway with water, wet both your finger and the rim of the glass, and run your finger along the rim, you would create your own vibrations.

Different vibrations have different frequencies, or tones. The less water in the glass, the higher the vibration sound. Most people can hear vibrations between 20 and 20,000 hertz (Hz). The lowest tone on the piano vibrates at 27.5 Hz, while the highest is at 4,186 Hz.

Vibrations, as we saw during our explorations of both the reptilian brain and our brains' own wave patterns, enter our bodies, affecting us. High-frequency sounds (3,000–6,000 Hz), made by instruments such as the violin, tend to resonate in our brain and affect cognitive functions. Middle-frequency sounds (750–3,000 Hz), like those of a clarinet, generally stimulate the heart, the lungs, and the emotions. Physical movement is affected by low-frequency sounds (below 750 Hz). Low-frequency drones make us groggy, whereas low, fast rhythms make it difficult to concentrate or be still.[1]

Music Note 18

Audio frequencies affect humans:
♪ High-frequency sounds affect cognitive functions.
♪ Middle-frequency sounds stimulate the heart, the lungs, and the emotions.
♪ Low-frequency sounds affect physical movement.

The octave. Some vibrations sound to the casual listener as if they are the same note. They are, in fact, the most basic unit of sound, the octave. An octave occurs when a frequency is doubled or halved. Middle C, for instance, has a frequency of 440 Hz, whereas high C has a frequency of 220 Hz. Probably the most common example of an octave is the difference in pitch between the female and male voice. The female voice is, in fact, one octave higher than the male voice.

The Octave

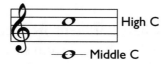

Different societies and cultures have all independently recognized this octave relationship as a fundamental acoustical fact.[2] The complications and variations occur when humans divide the frequencies between an octave into individual notes. These arbitrary divisions create scales.

Many different systems have resulted. For example:

- Australian Aborigines use a two-tone scale.
- Many non-Western cultures, including those in the Far East and Africa, limit their scales to five tones.
- Six-tone scales have been used in Western music by Debussy.
- Most Western music uses twelve-tone scales.
- India ragas are in twenty-two-tone scales.
- Twenty-four-tone scales are the norm in the Middle East.[3]

Music Note 19

Most Western music divides the octave into twelve notes.

Each of these tonal systems has a different sound and feeling. The intervals *between* the notes is what creates that music's characteristics. No one system is more natural than another. All scaling systems work within the context of their cultural framework and should be viewed within that context. *Training with a Beat: The Teaching Power of Music,* will primarily focus on the twelve-tone scale systems of Western music, for virtually all the music this book discusses is Western based.

Melodies. A second *American Heritage Collegiate Dictionary* definition of music is:

> Mu sic (myoo' zik) *n.* An aesthetically pleasing or harmonious sound or combination of sounds.[4]

The sounds exist, but they are not sufficient within themselves. They must be combined in such a way as to create a melody, for, in the words of musical scholar Victor Zuckerkandl, "A melody is a series of tones that make sense."[5] It is not the sound that causes the music; it is the relationship *between* those sounds that we hear as music.

Music Note 20

| It is the relationship between sounds we hear as music. |

Within the confines of an octave, tones have a tendency to suggest movement. Zuckerkandl, in *Music and the External World: Sound and Symbol,* suggests:

> We have understood the dynamic qualities of tone as the particular kind of unfulfillment peculiar to each tone, its desire for completion. No musical tone is sufficient unto itself; and as each musical tone points beyond itself, reaches, as it were, a hand to the next, so we too, as these hands reach out, listen tensely and expectantly for each new tone.[6]

Gian Carlo Menotti adds, "Melody is a form of remembrance. . . . It must have a quality of inevitability in our ears."[7]

The oldest known melodies are the Gregorian chants. These chants are some of the most majestic melodies ever created, and because of their melodiousness, they are still in use today.[8] In fact, many of the most successful composers of Western music are those who created the most pleasing melodies. Bach, Mozart, Beethoven, Bartok, Stravinsky, Ellington, Gershwin, and McCartney all were blessed with a gift for creating melodies that reverberate in the human brain and move our limbic system emotions.

Manuscript. An important step in the development of music was the creation of music manuscript, the documentation of the sounds that occur within a piece of music. Precise representations were essential for accurate repeat performances. Before melodic notation, singers learned music by oral tradition.[9] The oldest known manuscripts are from the ninth century. The notation in these documents is not precise, with the indication of pitch only approximated. They are an aid to the memory, not a record of the tones to be sung.

Around A.D. 1000 people began experimenting with multiple vocal parts. Memorizing one vocal part was difficult enough. Adding additional parts created layers of complexity and required a more effective notation system. By A.D. 1000 music manuscripts were being recorded in whatever system the transcriber, usually monks in monasteries, devised. This led to wide variations in notation, inconsistencies that mattered little in individual monasteries. A universal notation system did not become necessary until the invention of the printing press.

Movable type, although available in China for centuries, was first applied to Western music around 1475. The advent of printing type meant that music manuscript became less costly, less prone to copy error, more available, and preservable for later generations. It also forced a more uniform system of notation. By the 1600s our current notation system, with its series of bars and spaces naming different tones and their relationship to each other, was pretty much established. Effective facilitation does not require knowing this system. Paul McCartney, to name one famous composer, has created reams of memorable music without "reading" music.

Equal temperament. Once our current notation system was established, composers were then able to tackle another perplexing problem, intonation. Intonation, for our purposes, can be defined as the sounding relationship between simultaneously vibrating notes. Many different tuning systems had been devised and abandoned over the centuries. Perhaps the most important was the system devised by Greek mathematician Pythagoras.

Pythagoras believed that music was inseparable from numbers, which he thought to be the key to the spiritual and physical universe.[10] Pythagoras devoted most of his life to discovering and formalizing the mathematical relationships between the octave and various pitches. His formulas created an intonation system that lasted for hundreds of years.

Anicius Boethius, in *The Fundamentals of Music,* relates the way in which Pythagoras discovered the mathematical relationships that exist within an octave:

While passing the workshop of blacksmiths, he [Pythagoras] overheard the beating of hammers somehow emit a single consonance from differing sounds. Thus in the presence of what he had long sought, he approached the activity spellbound. Reflecting for a time, he decided that the strength of the men hammering caused the diversity of sounds, and in order to prove this more clearly, he commanded them to exchange hammers among themselves. But the property of sounds did not rest in the muscles of the men; rather, it followed the exchanged hammers. When he observed this, he examined the weight of the hammers. There happened to be five hammers, and those that sounded together the consonance of the octave were found to be double in weight. Pythagoras determined further that the one which weighed twice the second was in the ratio 3:4 with another, with which it sounded a fourth. Then he found that the same double of the second formed a ratio of 3:2 with still another, and that it joined with it in the consonance of the fifth.[11]

The intervals of the octave, fourth, and fifth that Pythagoras defined were mathematically correct. Musicians, following these formulas, would tune their instruments so that they vibrated in the correct octave, fourth, and fifth ratios. Music that concentrated on only these three frequencies sounded "in tune."

The exactness of this mathematical formulation made other notes sound funny, or "out of tune," when played together. The problem became especially difficult when musicians tried to perform pieces of music that centered on different notes than the ones tuned to the mathematical formula. The music became annoyingly out of tune and unbearable for listening.

As long as music used few notes and instruments, the intonation problem did not matter. Once composers, ever experimenting, began to expand musical techniques, something had to be done.

During the 1500s, a system called "equal temperament" began to evolve. Equal temperament was a logical compromise between the rich-sounding mathematical intervals and the practical needs of musicians. All the notes between an octave were arbitrarily and equally divided with a frequency ratio of 1.05946 between each tone. Musicians surrendered the richer sounds of pure tones, but gained an increased ability to perform in any key. The movement to equal temperament was completed with the publication of J. S. Bach's "Das Wohltemperierte Klavier" ("The Well-Tempered Clavier"). Bach wrote a different piece of music for each of the twenty-four keys, effectively demonstrating the practicality of this equal temperament system.[12] With the acceptance of this compromise, music performance was made practical and most of the music we know today could be created.

Major and minor keys. It is important to understand two different kinds of keys, major and minor. For, in the words of Ferruccio Busconi, "We teach four-and-twenty keys; but in fact, we have at our command only two, the major key and the minor key. The rest are merely transpositions."[13] The major-minor system is not a naturally occurring phenomenon in nature. Rather, it evolved out of musical practice over hundreds of years, eventually becoming our musical standard.[14]

Major keys have a happy feeling. They are the optimistic keys, creating positive-sounding music. Most rock music is in positive keys, as are most marches. Fast major-key music helps learning by cooling the brain, encouraging better moods.[15]

Minor keys have a sad feeling, giving the music a reflective sound. Reflective waltzes, some classical music, and pop ballads use minor keys. Minor keys did not exist until the Renaissance and did not come into wide usage until the Baroque period.[16] It is fortunate for the musical facilitator that they did. Slower music in minor keys is reported to warm the brain, making it more alert.[17] This attribute makes minor key music a major resource for learning experiences.

Music Note 21

Major keys sound happy; minor keys sound sad:
♪ *Major-key music cools the brain, encouraging better moods.*
♪ *Minor-key music warms the brain, making it more alert.*

Although, as we have established, the major-minor system is not a natural phenomenon, people appear to comprehend the emotional content of the music regardless of culture, education, and upbringing. In one study, children consistently interpreted emotions based on the major-minor focus of the music. They also associated major key, high-rhythmic activity, and staccato articulation with "happy" feelings and minor key, slow pulse, and low-rhythmic activity with "sad" emotions.[18] For learning purposes, the higher the pitch, the more positive the effect generated.[19] This information is not to imply that people outside the Western musical tradition would make the same associations. The study should be viewed in a cultural context.

With regard to that cultural context, our next chapter, "Musical Styles," will explore the different musical traditions of Western classical music and the proper training placement for that music.

Notes

1. Campbell, D. (1997). *The Mozart Effect: tapping the power of music to heal the body, strengthen the mind, and unlock the creative spirit.* New York: Avon Books.

2. *The 1995 Grolier Multimedia Encyclopedia.* (1995). vr. 7.0.2. Grolier Electronic Publishing, Inc.

3. *The New College Encyclopedia of Music.* (1999). New York: W.W. Norton & Company.

4. *The American Heritage Collegiate Dictionary,* 3rd ed. (1997). Boston: Houghton Mifflin Company.

5. Zuckerkandl, V. (1956). *Music and the External World: sound and symbol.* London: Routledge & Kegan Paul.

6. Ibid.

7. Menotti, G., quoted in *Webster's Dictionary of Quotations.* (1995). New York: Smithmark Publishers.

8. Grout, D., and Palisca, C. (1996). *A History of Western Music,* 5th ed. New York: W.W. Norton & Company.

9. Ibid.

10. Ibid.

11. Boethius, *The Fundamentals of Music* (1989), trans. with introduction and notes by Bower, C. New Haven: Yale University Press, as quoted in Grout, D., and Palisca, C. (1996).

12. Grout, D., and Palisca, C. (1996).

13. Busoni, F. (1992). *Three Classics in the Aesthetics of Music.* New York: Dover.

14. Grout, D., and Palisca, C. (1996).

15. Howard, P. (1994). *The Owner's Manual for the Brain: everyday applications from mind-brain research.* Austin: Leornian Press.

16. Meyer, L. (1956). *Emotion and Meaning in Music.* Chicago: University of Chicago Press.

17. Howard, P. (1994).

18. Kratus, J., reported in *MuSICA Research Notes,* II/1 (Spring 1995). <www.musica.uci.edu>.

19. Howard, P. (1994).

Chapter 10

MUSICAL STYLES

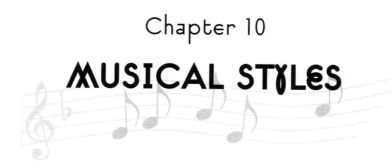

Music is the supreme expression of universal emotions, in an entirely personal way, by the great composers.

—Deryck Cooke

Effective placement of music in learning environments requires a basic familiarity with different musical styles. Because of music's elusiveness to most nonmusicians, this chapter will focus largely on classical music and what a trainer needs to know about it. We will then quickly overview other styles of music useful to the training beat.

WESTERN CLASSICAL MUSIC

Western classical music is loosely defined as historical cultural music of the Western civilization begun in Greece and spread by the Roman Empire.[2] "Historical culture music" sounds deceptively pompous. Think instead of Western music as a continuous long-term experiment in new sound creation. The music began with vocal songs, chants, and prayers. Over the sweep of time, composers and performers added new elements. With the creation of reliable instruments during the 1700s, instrumental music began to receive equal attention to vocal music.[3] Composers experimented with different instrumental combinations, new key signatures, and unusual meters. They intentionally established norms of composition. Then, just as intentionally, they broke, rewrote, and rebroke those norms. Each additional refinement encouraged more experimentation. As a composer introduced a new feature, other composers would add to and expand on that feature, adding more complexity. This slowly evolving, dynamic, almost alive, musical dialogue continues to this day, with the addition of electronic technologies and assimilation of nontraditional musical styles and norms.

It is difficult to accurately place Western classical music into historical categories. Just as meter is an arbitrary representation of time, so to is the historical record. Composers did not meet, discuss, and select names for each new period. Historians, with the advantage of time, have placed the composers into some generally agreed-upon eras. Let us begin with an overview of those eras.

Western Music Periods

Period	Dates	Type of Music	Composers
Medieval	Pre-1450	Gregorian Chant - sacred music, vocals, no instrumentation	van Bingen, Loenin, Perotin
Renaissance	1450–1600	More secular, counterpoint, complex harmonies, chansons	Desprez, Dowland, Tallis
Baroque	1600–1750	Music of intense passion and rigid uniformity	J. S. Bach, Vivaldi
Classical	1750–1820	Elegant, flexible, melodic, balanced, expressing multiple emotions	Beethoven, Haydn, Mozart
Early Romantic	1820–1860	Intense and personal, sweeping melodies, dynamic contrasts, extended forms, return to the dreamlike feel of the baroque period	Beethoven, Berlioz, Chopin, Liszt, Mendelssohn, Schumann
Late Romantic	1860–1900	Bolder, bigger, louder, adventurous	Brahms, Bruckner, Tchaikovsky, Wagner
Twentieth Century	1900–2000	New chromatic scales, tonalities, mediums; Debussy Impressionism, Gershwin jazz, Bartók dissonance, Babbitt experimentation, Glass minimalism, Schoenberg anti-tonalities	Babbitt, Bartók, Debussy, Gershwin, Glass, Ravel, Schoenberg

SOURCE: Grout, D., and Palisca, C. (1996). *A History of Western Music,* 5th ed. New York: W.W. Norton & Company.

Early/Medieval Music

Early and Medieval (pre-1450) music is, by and large, not useful in learning situations. The musical instruments we are familiar with today were in their infancy during this time period, so instrumental music of the era sounds crude by today's standards. In addition, most of the music is vocal based, making it even less helpful. Gregorian chant for instance, has a pensive, reflective quality useful for meditation and study, but the vocals can sometimes be intrusive.

Renaissance Music

Renaissance (1450–1600) composers included Josquin Desprez, John Dowland, and Hildegard von Bingen. Renaissance music is more developed than Medieval music, but it still has an infancy quality about it. Many of the selections are vocal and thus are not appropriate for most training situations. Some of the music, however, especially the instrumental music of composers like John Dowland, can be effectively used for reflection.

Baroque Music

The word *Baroque* actually means abnormal, grotesque, or in bad taste. 1920s art critics Jacob Burckhardt and Karl Baedeker applied the term to the music written between 1600 and 1750.[4] In spite of that label, Baroque music is perhaps the best source of learning music. People of the era believed emotions were states of the soul. Composers sought to bring forth universal feelings through their music while simultaneously keeping their individual emotions out of the composition. The result was a music either very free flowing or extremely steady in tone and temperament, and simultaneously objective and passionate.[5] Its clarity of form and finely chiseled features make it an ideal music for learning applications. Most Baroque music pulses between 76 to 80 beats per minute, paralleling the human heartbeat and the brain's relaxed Alpha and Theta wavelengths.[6] It has the ability to be both moving and intellectual, appealing to the limbic system and the neocortex.

Two Baroque composers bear special mention: Antonio Vivaldi and Johann Sebastian Bach.

Antonio Vivaldi. Vivaldi, a full-fledged priest, was the first composer to make the slow movements in his compositions as important as faster movements. His music has a useful sameness and a melodic richness best illustrated by his masterpiece, The Four Seasons. The sameness comes about from the feeling of continuity and repetition in his music. In fact, it was joked that Vivaldi wrote the same piece of music 450 times.[7] Fortunately, the melodic richness of the music overpowers its repetitiveness. His melodies are so pleasing that they bear repeating over and over. In addition, for music applications, the sameness helps Vivaldi's music become a background to learning.

Johann Sebastian Bach. Bach led an uneventful life, devoting himself to his church and to God.[8] During his life, Bach was a well-known musical craftsman, but he was not highly widely regarded as a composer in his time. His work was quickly forgotten once he died. Even so, there was something eternal to Bach's music. Copies of Bach's manuscripts were in continuous circulation throughout Europe. Even Mozart studied Bach! In 1850, the Bach Society was established, leading to the publication of Bach's works in 1900. Bach's popularity continues to grow. Two hundred years after his death, the complete works of Bach are available for purchase and rank among classical music's best-selling titles.

In hindsight, Bach's music is widely regarded for its "concentrated and distinct themes, musical invention, the balance between harmonic and contrapuntal forces, the strength of his rhythmic drive, the clarity of form, the grand proportions, his imaginative use of pictorial and symbolic figures, the intensity of expression always controlled by a ruling architectural idea, and the technical perfection of every detail."[9] This unusual balance in all areas makes Bach's music extremely helpful learning material. It engages the entire brain, left and right, with its technical perfection appealing to the left hemisphere, and its emotionality engaging the right hemisphere.

George Frideric Handel and Franz Joseph Haydn. Many music lovers enjoy the works of George Frideric Handel (Baroque period) and Franz Joseph Haydn (Classical period). To be candid, I find the music lacking in melody, impersonal, and overly simplistic. Consequently, I do not use it. No insult to this great music is intended. Rather, it is a matter of personal preference based on experience. If you like the music, and your learners respond to it, then you can, and should, use it, as appropriate for your needs.

Classical Music

Some of the most popular music ever written comes from the Classical period (1750–1820). The works of Wolfgang Amadeus Mozart, and the early compositions of Ludwig van Beethoven bear special examination.

Western Music Learning Usefulness

Period	Composers	Learning Usefulness
Medieval	van Bingen, Loenin, Perotin	Although vocal in nature, pensive, reflective quality makes it useful for meditation and study
Renaissance	Desprez, Dowland	Instrumental lute music for reflection and reading
Baroque	J. S. Bach, Vivaldi	Ideal for learning: Intense passionate and uniform, it is both moving and intellectual, reaching the limbic system and neocortex
Classical	Beethoven, Haydn, Mozart	Melodic nature useful for training; multiple moods within each piece make careful selection critical
Early Romantic	Beethoven, Berlioz, Chopin, Liszt, Mendelssohn, Schumann	Sweeping melodies, dynamic contrasts, extended forms make its use difficult; careful selection a must; useful for love, compassion, sharing
Late Romantic	Brahms, Bruckner, Tchaikovsky, Wagner	Bolder, bigger, louder, more adventurous; not useful for learning
Twentieth Century	Babbitt, Bartók, Debussy, Gershwin, Glass, Ravel, Schoenberg	Debussy Impressionism ideal for daydreaming and creative exercise; Gershwin useful for setting an urban mood; Stravinsky and others created jarring and dissonant music—avoid at all costs

Wolfgang Amadeus Mozart. Mozart was the bad boy "rock star" of his era. *Sex, Drink, and Sonatas* could have been the title of Mozart's biography. No mass media existed to create a persona for him. Mozart did not need the hype. He provided plenty of his own. From his debut as a composer and performer at age five, until his death on December 5, 1791, at the young age of thirty-six, Mozart was never healthy, but always demanding. Short, abrasive, loud, obnoxious, and extremely talented, Mozart enthralled, captivated, and enraged all who came in contact with him. He even, as a youngster, proposed marriage to the French queen Marie Antoinette![10]

Mozart's output of music was truly astonishing. He began composing at the age of five, and, by the time he died, had composed at least six hundred pieces of music.[11] Mozart admired and modeled Bach's usage of melodic themes and thematic contrasts. The music is complex, ambivalent, insightful, and extremely emotional. It teems with carefully crafted, extremely melodic phrases.[12] Its form appeals to the left hemisphere, while its emotion moves the right hemisphere. Mozart pieces that beat at a rate of 60 to 75 beats a minute can pull the brain into relaxed Alpha states. These features make Mozart's slower compositions the ideal learning music.

Ludwig van Beethoven. Beethoven, at seventeen, performed on the piano for Mozart. Mozart predicted a bright future for the young Beethoven. He was correct. Beethoven composed at least 340 works, spanning the Classical and Early Romantic periods. What makes his contribution even more remarkable is the fact that he composed many of his most famous works after he had become completely deaf.[13]

If Mozart was the rock star, then Beethoven was the moody, ill-tempered, arrogant, sought after, respected artist. In one memorable outburst, Beethoven shouted at a patron prince, "There are and there will be thousands of princes. There is only one Beethoven." Indeed, those who knew Beethoven appreciated that fact. Beethoven cared little about social niceties. Personal hygiene was not a priority. Rudeness was normal behavior. Beethoven would leave restaurants without paying his bill, perform only when he felt the mood, and insult any "ass" who crossed his path—usually everyone he met. Regardless, Beethoven's music was so well respected, that twenty thousand people attended his funeral![14] For learning applications, Beethoven's early classical music is most helpful.

Early Romantic Music

Early Romantic (1820–60) composers experimented with sweeping melodies and dynamic contrasts. As Beethoven matured and sank into a deafness-induced funk, his music became progressively more introspective and emotional. Beethoven's later works are almost violently moody, with sudden changes in feeling and volume. The constant shifting of dynamics renders this music a difficult fit for training, especially in situations where the music must remain background to learning.

Other Early Romantic composers, whose works are renowned, but equally useless for learning, include Hector Berlioz, Fryderyk Chopin, Franz Liszt, Felix Mendelssohn, and Robert Schumann.

Late Romantic Music

In the Late Romantic period (1860–1900), composers, inspired by Beethoven, experimented with bigger and bolder sounds. This music, including the works of Johannes Brahms, Anton Bruckner, Piotr Tchaikovsky, and Richard Wagner, although exciting, emotional, rambunctious, and enjoyable, can be largely ignored as a teaching tool, as can most Twentieth-Century music (1900–2000).

Twentieth-Century Music

In the continuous effort to create new sounds, twentieth-century composers, including Milton Babbitt, Béla Bartók, Philip Glass, Charles Ives, Maurice Ravel, Arnold Schoenberg, and Igor Stravinsky, abandoned much of the tradition that came before them. Gone were the major-minor tonalities, common meters, familiar scales, and standard instrumentation. The result is a wonderfully rich, but chaotic, music that can be difficult to apply in learning situations. Some of the music may be too draining, jarring, and dissonant, and require too much of your learners' attention. Use it only if you know the music well, and want the trainees to focus on the music.

Claude Debussy. One type of Twentieth-Century music that is applicable for learning is the Impressionistic music of Claude Debussy (1862–1918). This music is designed to capture pure moods. It is so dreamlike it floats.[15] The airiness of the music brings forth a relaxed Theta state, making it ideal for daydreaming and creative exercises.

George Gershwin and Aaron Copeland. Gershwin and Copeland composed music with a decidedly American sound. It may be appropriate in specific learning situations, but it is generally too specific in its sound.

There are, of course, many other composers and types of Classical music. This listing is intended as an overview of the most known and, therefore, most helpful learning music widely available. The intent of this listing is not to exclude other possibilities. You should, in fact, seek those out.

OTHER KINDS OF MUSIC

There are as many styles of music as there are peoples in the world. Each culture, age bracket, economic strata, and country has its own musical tradition. To discuss all of these variations would be nearly impossible, and would probably not be relevant. The teaching power of music comes from music that captures your learners and makes the points you want made. Your music selections should mirror your learners. As a general rule, the more mainstream the music you select, the more chance there is that every trainee will know the material and be able to find personal relevance in it. Within that context, we will discuss a few categories of music.

Those broad classifications are:

- Sound tracks
- Popular
- Jazz and blues
- New Age

Sound Tracks

Sound track recordings exist for virtually every musical, movie, and even some television shows, with each album containing a wealth of material. Of course, some of these selections are overly familiar. Those selections may be useful, but be warned. Your goal should be to enrich your training, not to remind someone of a movie they may have enjoyed or disliked. Some movie themes become so popular they have little training currency.

There are, however, specific situations in which a movie theme can be useful. Movie and Broadway musicals are great sources for specific songs about specific situations. Musicals have been recorded about everything from baseball to politics, to gang warfare, to union agitation. If a musical recording has been made on a subject relating to your training topic, the recording may serve as a metaphor, or as a framing device for discussion.

Sound track recordings are most helpful—not for the material your learners already know, but for the instrumental material tucked into the folds of the recording—the instrumental tracks that were written and recorded for the movie. People may have heard these selections before, but they will rarely recognize them, except in the most obscure, "I've heard that somewhere before" fashion. The advantage this material offers is that it was written to capture and encourage a specific mood on the screen. These selections can be strategically placed within the folds of your training to foster a mood you need at that moment.

Finding appropriate sound track mood music is pretty simple. As you watch a movie, pay attention with your ears. When you are feeling a strong emotion in the theater—anger, excitement, love, laughter, whimsy, or whatever—listen to the music playing behind the action. If you responded to the mood of the music in a manner similar to the rest of the theater audience, the chances are excellent that the music will replicate that mood in your training environment.

Popular

This broad category includes top forty, country, easy listening, rap, and rhythm and blues. The radio play lists of the last fifty years have many training applications. Certainly advertisers believe in the power of music.

Upbeat popular songs coax viewer brains into Beta states, making them more alert and receptive to a commercial's message. Music is so critical a tool for making that connection that advertisers pay exorbitant sums, up to $4 million, for the rights to use a song in their ads. *USA Today* reported that commercials incorporating well-known songs are among the most popular and successful.[16] There are numerous examples of pop music's effectiveness. In one notable instance, a Japanese car manufacturer, concerned that its cars were perceived as not American, placed country music songs in its ads. Within two years, the automobile was no longer regarded as "foreign."

Pop music, especially faster selections, is used extensively in movies. Movie producers have been reported to pay as much as $50,000 each to the publisher and the recording label. Such high fees are routinely generated because the music connects with viewers on a different level than the rest of the film, perhaps by amplifying the action, illuminating characters' feelings, or evoking a certain mood or time period.[17]

The most effective songs are those that are recognizable but not current. Current selections may invite unwanted thoughts and ideas, while years separate older material from the immediacy of everyday life. Older songs give you the advantage of familiarity, without the disadvantage of currency.

Some specific types of pop songs we should mention include country, rap, and rock. All three genres are predominately vocal music. For suggestions regarding the use of music with lyrics, please refer to chapter 12, "Teaching with Lyrics." Additional comments are, however, offered here for each of the three.

Rap is an emotionally angry music that will not calm your trainees down. Use it only if you want agitation. In addition, rap is predominately spoken. As such, it attracts a person's attention. Some of the same parameters apply to rock music. Although rock is not as hostile as rap, it does have a juvenile emotional edge to it. It is not helpful in reflective situations. It may, however, be appropriate when you want to increase energy levels, raising brain waves into Beta state and cooling the brain to create better moods. Country music projects a less violent emotion than both rap and rock, but, because of its vocal nature, it is almost useless for training.

Jazz and Blues

I studied at a leading jazz college, Berklee College of Music. I wish I could recommend the use of jazz favorites in the classroom. The reality, however, is that jazz is intended as an intellectual listening and per-forming music. It demands attention. Jazz was not meant to be back-ground, and it should not be placed in that position. If you use jazz or blues, place it in situations where the music is intentionally highlighted.

New Age

New Age music selections, especially those with minimal rhythm, slow down our brain waves to Alpha and Theta states, which help people relax. Many of the selections have a dreamlike quality that makes them ideal for brainstorming. Artists include Eyna, Yanni, George Winston, and Michael C. My caution about New Age music is that there is a lot of mediocre material on the market. Both pop and classical musics have the advantage of being time tested. You know it is of high quality, and so do your learners. Many New Age selections are unknown, render-ing the material less relevant for learning and requiring you to listen to great volumes of material to find worthwhile selections.

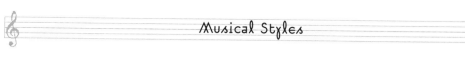

Music Note 22

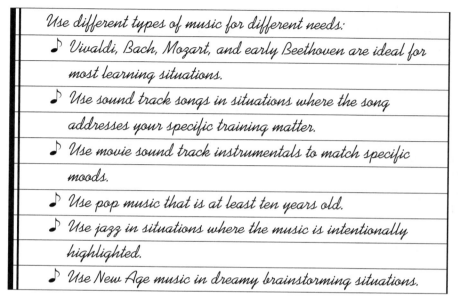

Use different types of music for different needs:

♪ Vivaldi, Bach, Mozart, and early Beethoven are ideal for most learning situations.

♪ Use sound track songs in situations where the song addresses your specific training matter.

♪ Use movie sound track instrumentals to match specific moods.

♪ Use pop music that is at least ten years old.

♪ Use jazz in situations where the music is intentionally highlighted.

♪ Use New Age music in dreamy brainstorming situations.

Finally, consider two filters for selecting the best music:

First, the best songs are those that have both clarity of form and purpose.

Music Note 23

The best songs are those that have both clarity of form and purpose.

A well-designed song should not leave you confused. It should tell a story or capture a mood so completely that you instinctually know the song's meaning. If the song feels right to you within the context of your training subject, then it is a good choice for your class.

Second, use Mozart's perfect balance of emotion and intellect as a guideline. A helpful training song should maintain a constant tempo and volume level, feature consistent instrumentation, and not draw attention to itself.

Music Note 24

Following the "Mozart Music Meter," training music should:
♪ maintain a constant tempo
♪ maintain a constant volume level
♪ feature consistent instrumentation
♪ not draw attention to itself

If the song does all of these things, use it with assurance.

Now that we have a clearer understanding of the musical styles available, we will begin placing different compositions in their proper training context. In our next chapter, we will join Jerleen as she explores "Teaching with Music."

Notes

1. Cooke, D. (1959). *The Language of Music*. London: Oxford University Press.

2. Grout, D., and Palisca, C. (1996). *A History of Western Music*, 5th ed. New York: W.W. Norton & Company.

3. Ibid.

4. Ibid.

5. Ibid.

6. Iwanaga, M. "Relationship between Heart Beat and Preference for Tempo in Music." *Perceptual and Motor Skills*, 81/2 (1995): 435–40.

7. Barber, D. (1986). *Bach, Beethoven, and the Boys: music as it ought to be taught*, 10th anniversary ed. Toronto: Sound and Vision.

8. Ibid.

9. Grout, D., and Palisca, C. (1996).

10. Barber, D. (1986).

11. Koechel, L. (1964). *Thematic Catalog,* vr. 6, Alfred Einstein, ed. Wiesbaden, Germany: Breitkopf & Hartel.

12. Grout, D., and Palisca, C. (1996).

13. Ibid.

14. Barber, D. (1986).

15. Grout, D., and Palisca, C. (1996).

16. Well, M. *USA Today,* May 24, 1999.

17. *Chicago Tribune,* October 24, 1999.

Part Three

MUSIC

Explained

Explored

Applied

Music, when soft voices die,
vibrates in the memory.
—Percy Bysshe Shelley

Chapter 11

TEACHING WITH MUSIC

The Continuing
Adventures of Jerleen
Part One

*Jerleen was worried. As the old song said, "bad luck, that's what I got," she thought. The training department assigned classes by the most rudimentary manner—drawing from a hat. "Remind me to hide that hat," she muttered. She was scheduled to teach diversity (of all things!) to the all-male, all-white, maintenance department (of all places!). "How do you expect an African-American woman to reach them?" she asked her boss. "Anything I say will sound preachy." The boss would not listen. "Isn't that what diversity is all about," she asked, "using **all** of our trainers equally?" Well, damn, she was right; not smart, but right.*

Jerleen had met these men before. One time, when she was new to the firm, she had entered their turf. What a mistake. They ignored her by turning up the radio. She eventually got what she wanted, but the experience was not worth repeating. All her subsequent contacts with them had been through the anonymity of a phone. If only she could train by phone.

She would need to be creative to survive tomorrow. She spent most of the day and the evening searching for ways to overcome the men's hostility. It was around midnight when the answer came. The radio. She would use music.

We have established how triune brain theory, left-right hemispherization, multiple and emotional intelligences, and brain waves all relate to music. Now we will apply the musical aspects of these theories to learning environments. We begin with an exploration of instrumental music, for most learning activities require nonverbal music. In chapter 12, "Teaching with Lyrics," we will focus on vocal music.

Instrumental music is applicable in many learning situations. Music:

- establishes a positive learning environment
- minimizes negative conditions surrounding a subject
- creates a metaphor for the task to be learned
- provides background sound
- assists with repeated tasks
- aids memorization
- transports your learners to different times and locales
- enhances reviews
- frames games and activities
- changes energy levels
- fosters creativity
- provides closure

Music Establishes a Positive Learning Environment

People are often uncomfortable entering the learning environment. In their book, *The Creative Trainer: Holistic Facilitation Skills for Accelerated Learning*, Michael Lawlor and Peter Handley commented, "Most people have been conditioned by their home or school environment to believe that their memory, their creativity, and their overall ability are limited"[1]:

- Learning requires admitting knowledge gaps—in front of strangers, in an unfamiliar room, to facilitators not yet met. No wonder participants fear learning.

- People remember negative school experiences. Unfortunately, the training room reminds learners of boring classes, pompous teachers, punishment and embarrassment, mindless facts, and a loss of personal control. These adults are convinced they cannot learn.[2] This lack of confidence is so ingrained that it prevents knowledgeable adults—people who have raised families, bought houses, and navigated the career world— from returning to school for additional education.

- Older people sometimes doubt their own abilities, thinking the world has passed them by. They believe they are slow to learn, and they fear embarrassment.

- Some people think they are too busy to learn. Crossing items off the daily checklist is their priority. Learning time means postponing instant checklist gratification, while wasting time in potentially irrelevant learning experiences.

- Employee suspicion about company and management motives can also block learning. A suspicious "What are they trying to force on me now" attitude is not conducive to learning.

Fortunately, none of these difficulties are insurmountable. Psychologist Raymond Wlodkowski, in his book, *Enhancing Adult Motivation to Learn*, reports, "The first time people experience anything that is new or that occurs in a different setting, they form an impression that will have a lasting impact."[3] In his adult learning Andragogy model, Malcolm Knowles stated that a climate of adultness is a critical prefix to learning.[4] Your learners should experience a positive, accepting, adult learning climate the moment they enter your training room. The environment you establish should be an irresistible invitation to learn.[5] Music familiar to the learners, or appropriate to the learning environment, can establish this climate.

Knowles also believed that learners have to want to learn. Adult learning researcher Edward Thorndike captured this concept in his Law of Readiness, stating that "if an organism is ready for a meaningful connection to the learning, then learning will be enhanced, otherwise learning is inhibited."[6] Music reaches past the thinking brain, into the emotions of your learners, disarming antilearning defenses. Leonard Meyer agreed: "Music activates tendencies, inhibits them, and provides meaningful and relevant resolutions."[7] Music is a relaxer. It creates better moods, happier thoughts, and greater relaxation.[8]

> Music has charms to soothe a savage beast,
> To soften rocks, or bend a knotted oak.[9]
> —William Congreve

The brain's limbic system, acting as the memory controller, will filter all incoming information, including information about your training event. Providing pleasant emotional content to your learners will establish a link between you, your classroom, and the learners' pleasure. It will make your learning environment feel emotionally "right" and free from negative associations. Learners who walk into your classroom and immediately feel comfortable because of the music you play will be engaged to learn. Their limbic system will send the signal that this environment is safe. The learning will be irresistible.

Music Minimizes Negative Conditions Surrounding a Subject

People can react with extreme negativity to some subjects. Wlodkowski suggests that when subjects with unpleasant emotions are present, the learner will slip into an avoidance mode.[10] Most trainers have experienced the uncomfortable situation where learners decided in advance not to cooperate and refused to learn. Music can transcend intellectual learning blocks by reaching deeper—into the limbic system, creating Alpha or Theta states. "Arthur Schopenhauer believed that music was the incarnation of innermost reality, the immediate expression of universal feelings and impulses in concrete, definite form."[11] A fast, major-key piece of music that relates to the subject being taught will bring forth a Beta state, placing your learners in a better mood. They will open up to the learning in spite of their hostility.

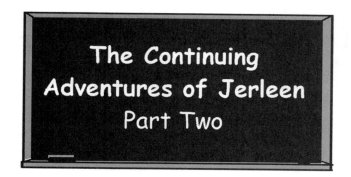

The Continuing
Adventures of Jerleen
Part Two

Jerleen was determined to hide her apprehension, but she was tired and nervous. She stood in the hall and greeted the men as they approached. Their posture indicated they obviously did not want to be here. It would be a long day. Fortunately, Jerleen knew she had the edge. The radio station the men listened to was an "oldies" station; the kind that plays late fifties to early sixties music. Jerleen had rummaged through her collection and found an audiocassette of the oldies music. As the men entered the training room, the music hit them.

Once all the men had arrived, late of course, Jerleen asked them to introduce themselves, name their favorite oldies song, and state why that song was favored. To model the behavior she sought, she introduced herself first and named a song from the tape.

Halfway through the introductions the melting began. One remembered high school, one talked about his brother, one had sung in a band, and one had even proposed marriage, all to songs. When the introductions were over, she asked if anyone knew the origins of the songs they had named. A few did. Rock and roll had resulted from a combining of European classical and folk melodies with the African chanting-rhythmic tradition. It was a marriage of cultures. "Can you imagine the world without these songs?" she asked. Of course they could not, and she had won. "Without diversity," she exclaimed, "there would be no music to remember." As she began to discuss the class objectives, she thought to herself, "Jerleen, you are smooth."

Music Creates a Metaphor for the Task to Be Learned

> Significant learning combines the logical and
> the intuitive, the intellect and the feelings, the
> concept and the meaning. When we learn in
> that way, we are whole.[12]
>
> —Carl Rogers

Metaphors are created when one item is compared to another in such a way as to make the concept of the first item more understandable. Gabriele Lusser Rico described metaphors as "word pictures that give language power and richness by involving our senses in the experience."[13] When people say things like "smooth as silk," or "fast as lightning," or "the left hand doesn't know what the right hand is doing," they are repeating metaphors. A metaphor's usefulness derives from its ability to make a seemingly difficult concept understandable. Adults have accumulated a depth of experience that serves as a framework for new learning.[14] Metaphors tap into that reservoir. Wlodkowski recommends using metaphors to help learners gain personal understanding of the subject being taught. "If we can assist learners to see, hear, or feel an idea, we substantially increase their engagement."[15]

Many pieces of music tell great metaphorical stories. The musical trainer is one who knows a song's meaning and can tie that meaning into the subject being taught.

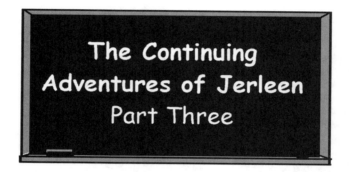

The Continuing
Adventures of Jerleen
Part Three

Once she had explained the class objectives, Jerleen looked around. They were paying attention. Her next activity would make them hers. "Let's continue with our musical theme. I want to play one more song for you. Listen to it. Pay special attention to its meaning." The next thing the men heard was Randy Newman's funny antibigotry song, "Short People," with the lyric proclaiming that short people should not live.

Music Provides Background Sound

Background music during learning discussions and solo reflection activities can be especially helpful. Background music:

- creates a "dedicated and concentrated mood,"[16] producing Alpha frequencies for concentration or Beta waves for alertness[17]

- creates a sense of privacy for small group discussion, making conversations more satisfying[18] and your learners more likely to say what they feel[19]
- enters into memory and aids recall
- masks ambient noise from other groups, machinery, or instructor preparation activities

The steady tones and tempos of Baroque music make it ideal for this purpose. Much of it was in fact composed as background music for kings, emperors, and other dignitaries.

The Continuing Adventures of Jerleen Part Four

When the song completed its mock hostility to short people, Jerleen divided the men into groups based on height, and asked each group to discuss the song's meaning. For background music during the discussion, she selected a slow Mozart work, "Concerto No. 2 in D Major, Andante." She walked around the room in amazement. They were focused on the lyrics of the Newman song. Gradually, it occurred to the men how ridiculous the song was. They began to kid each other about who was the shortest, expressing mock dislike for tall, fat, old, and young people. Of course she'd have to stop that, but that would come next. The important point was that they were loosening up and close to accepting the concept of diversity.

Once the men had dissected the lyrics, they engaged in a surprisingly fruitful discussion. The opinions offered captured just the tone Jerleen needed—humorously serious. Not one of them agreed that short people were inferior. The timing was perfect. Jerleen could now teach the company's diversity policy.

Music Assists with Repeated Tasks

When soldiers march, they sing. Walking requires rhythm, as does breathing, the heartbeat, and any repeated task. Throughout the world, people organize and perform repetitive work to music. From boat rowing to fruit picking, to assembly line work, to jogging, people synchronize music with repetitive movements because it works.

Music with a beat helps trainees:

- repeat monotonous tasks with a higher level of interest[20]

- work longer and faster through an increased attention span, increasing both speed and task longevity with the addition of music[21]

- focus on the task at hand, improving task concentration by alleviating anxiety[22]

- build consistency and increase speed

Any activity with a timed sequence can be set to music. For example, store checkout scanning, fast food preparation and cooking, shelf stocking, or any manufacturing procedure that requires repeated tasks can be learned in time with music. Once consistency has been established, accelerating the musical tempo can help your learners gain speed.

Music Note 25

Music with a beat helps trainees:
♪ *repeat monotonous tasks with a higher level of interest*
♪ *work longer and faster*
♪ *focus on the task at hand*
♪ *build consistency and increase speed*

Music Aids Memorization

Words and music, when tied together, engage both the left and right hemispheres of the brain, harnessing more of your trainees' brainpower. A famous 1967 Lee Marvin movie, *The Dirty Dozen,* featured a story line in which hardened convicts were pressed into service for a suicide mission during World War II. The tasks the men had to accomplish required a specific, complicated sequence. To help these men of limited schooling learn the correct task order, the entire team chanted the sequence of events. You may not have to fight a world war in your learning environment, but your trainees' ability to memorize complicated material will increase dramatically with this technique.

Music Transports Your Learners to Different Times and Locales

Music can transport your learners to a different environment. Schopenhauer, in *The World as Will and Representation,* explains, "When music suitable to any scene, action, event, or environment is played, it seems to disclose to us its most secret meaning, and appears to be the most accurate and distinct commentary on it."[23] Transporting music establishes the appropriate mood for a host of learning applications, from cultural familiarizations to food- and wine-tasting situations. Music that sounds "bluesy" can suggest a big city environment, down home harmonica music can suggest the American West, Chinese music can transport your learners to the Orient, movie music can set a show business theme, and Renaissance music can place your learners in sixteenth-century England for a Shakespeare reading.

Music Enhances Reviews

As we saw during chapter 7, "Music and Learning," noted educational psychologist Georgi Lozanov created a learning theory he called "suggestopedia." The power of suggestopedia lies in its ability to tap into the "reserve powers of the brain, located in the subconscious," and harness those powers through the use of suggestion while the brain is in an Alpha or a Theta state.[24] Accelerated learning theory is in large part based on Dr. Lozanov's methods, and it has helped people learn as much as ten times faster, while experiencing greater recall.[25] There are many elements to suggestopedia, but the one that concerns us is the "Passive Concert."

During a passive concert, slow Baroque or early Classical period music, pulsing at a rate parallel to that of the human heart, around 60 to 80 beats per minute, is employed. This music helps decrease brain activity and create a relaxed Alpha state of awareness. Once sufficient time had passed for the learners to reach Alpha state, Lozanov would recite, almost hypnotically, key learning points. Trainers can use this technique before quizzes, as a recap at the end of learning modules, and as a refresher after breaks. Passive concerts can be especially useful in that supposedly sleepy time after lunch when the body is tired, but the mind is alert.

The Continuing
Adventures of Jerleen
Part Five

The lecture was over. It was time to review. "I want to help you memorize this material in the easiest way possible," Jerleen said, "Let's try a review. I'm going to play some soft music. As the music plays, I'll repeat some of the terms we have discussed. All you have to do is sit back, relax, and enjoy the music." Jerleen played Mozart's Clarinet Concerto in A, Adagio, and the passive concert began.

Music Frames Games and Activities

Wlodkowski suggests that adult motivation to learn is enhanced when teachers introduce, connect, and end learning activities attractively and clearly.[26] Any learning activity can be tied to appropriate musical themes. For example, game shows allow trainers to test material in a nonthreatening manner. Themed music frames such activities, making them less testlike and more enjoyable.

Use themed music to:

- Introduce the topic. Musical game show themes are easily recognizable. Their use creates a game-playing environment.

- Establish expectations. Music that establishes expectations for the next activity saves time. If your learners are familiar with the game to be played, they will know the concept and rules immediately upon hearing the theme music.

110

- Set time limits. When a learner must answer a question within a specific time period, a short music clip can serve as the timekeeper.

- End the activity. Repeating the opening theme at the conclusion of the activity provides a finality, signaling the end of the activity.

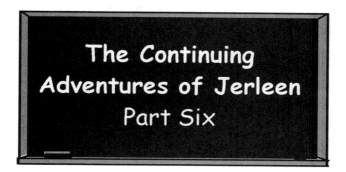

The session was half done, and no one had left. Even better, the men were attentive. It was time to check for comprehension. Jerleen chose a game she had used many times—a television game show parody. Several months back, she had purchased trainer's music with game show sounds, and she used that now as she hyped, in her best announcer's voice, that it was time to play the "Diversiwicz Family Face-Off."

Music Changes Energy Levels

Music can change the dynamic of your learning environment at appropriate moments, encouraging people to move about, relax, calm down, or get excited, depending on the needs of your session. One study found that people associated the emotion "excited" with high-rhythmic activity in $\frac{3}{4}$ and "calm" with low-rhythmic activity in $\frac{4}{4}$.[27] Loud, fast music can increase brain waves and encourage increased nervous system activity, while slow music can slow brain activity, helping people relax.[28]

Music Note 26

Use the tempo of the music to change energy levels:
♪ High-rhythmic activity in ¾ excites people.
♪ Low-rhythmic activity in ⁴⁄₄ calms people.
♪ Fast, major-key music encourages better learning moods.
♪ Slow music helps people relax.

People also consistently ascribe specific emotions to music. A study conducted by John Kratus of Case Western Reserve University demonstrated that people associate:

- fast music featuring high-rhythmic activity and short, quick notes with a "happy" mood
- slow pieces of music featuring low-rhythmic activity with "sad" moods
- high-rhythmic activity in ¾ with "excited" moods
- low-rhythmic activity in ⁴⁄₄ with "calm" moods

This information is useful in a number of ways. Use music to focus the mood you need and maintain control over the learning environment:

- After intense concentration, play faster music in a major key to encourage better moods.
- After heated discussion, play slow, minor-key music with low-rhythmic activity to calm your learners down.
- After a depressing, worrisome discussion, play major-key music with high-rhythmic activity and short, quick notes to create a "happy" mood.

- When the learners are bored, play music that has high-rhythmic activity in $\frac{3}{4}$ to boost excitement levels.
- To calm aggressive tendencies, play minor-key music with low-rhythmic activity in $\frac{4}{4}$.

The Continuing Adventures of Jerleen Part Seven

The Diversiwicz Family Face-Off game was a huge success. Now that Jerleen had checked for retention, she knew the participants understood company policy. Better yet, they were having fun. Maybe a little too much she thought. The adrenaline was so high that no one would be able to concentrate. Jerleen called a short break. For break music, she selected a dreamy New Age minor-key selection in $\frac{4}{4}$, Yanni's "Once Upon a Time." By the time the session resumed, the adrenaline level had subsided as the men floated with the music.

Music Fosters Creativity

Music enhances our creativity.[29] Anthony Storr, in *Music and the Mind,* stated, "Music plays a special role in aiding the scanning and sorting process which goes on when we are asleep [in Theta state] or simply day-dreaming."[30] Cathy McKinney and Frederick Tims proved that "classical music is especially useful in that it intensifies the ability of both people, regardless of their visualizing ability, to be creative."[31]

Brainstorming sessions are an ideal place to use music, allowing your participants to develop and link material in connecting applications.[32] Music that brings your learners' brain waves into Theta state will focus their creativity and will give their brainstorms anchors to attach to.

The Continuing
Adventures of Jerleen
Part Eight

Jerleen called the class to order by turning off the music. "Now that we know the company's diversity policy, what can you do to apply it?" she asked. "I will give you two minutes to discuss this question at your table." She played Debussy's "Clair de lune" to help them brainstorm. The discussion was going so well that she let the piece play for its full four minutes. She thought to herself, "This is too easy."

Music Provides Closure

Wlodkowski reports, "For people all over the world, festivals and holidays have been a joyous means of acknowledging the ending of seasons, religious periods, and harvests."[33] Harvard sociobiologist Edward O. Wilson, in *Sociobiology*, explains, "Singing and dancing serve to draw groups together, direct the emotions of the people, and prepare them for joint action."[34] The completion of any learning activity or session is a cause for celebration. Something important has been accomplished. Enjoy the moment with your learners. "Celebrations," according to

Wlodkowski, "allow people to feel pleasure for whatever they personally accomplished or valued during the entire learning process."[35]

Music is an ideal companion to celebrations. It helps frame a closing ceremony, making the closure more notable. Graduation music can be used for handing out diplomas and dance music can suggest a celebratory party.

Music Note 27

Music can be used to:
♪ establish a positive learning environment
♪ minimize negative conditions surrounding a subject
♪ create a metaphor for the task to be learned
♪ provide background sound
♪ assist with repeated tasks
♪ aid memorization
♪ transport your learners to different times and locales
♪ enhance reviews
♪ frame games and activities
♪ change energy levels
♪ foster creativity
♪ provide closure

For additional information pertaining to instrumental music placement in learning situations, see the appendices.

The Continuing
Adventures of Jerleen
Part Nine

When the music ended, Jerleen called the group to order and asked them to report out. The suggestions and comments they offered were worthwhile. This class was one to celebrate. To thank them for their participation, she had prepared certificates of merit. As she distributed the certificates, she played a Kool and the Gang's dance hit, "Celebration." What a difference an hour made. Whereas they had entered the room full of hostility and intimidation, they practically danced their way out.

That should have been the end of Jerleen's encounter with Maintenance. Fortunately for her, it was not. When she arrived at her office the next day, she realized that someone from Maintenance had visited *her* turf. On her desk, tied in a bow, was an old, scratched 45 RPM record. It was the song Jerleen had named as her favorite. On the label, someone had written, "I give your class a '10.' It had a beat."

Notes

1. Lozanov, G. (1978). *Suggestology and Outlines of Suggestopedy*. New York: Gordon and Breach; Lawlor, M., and Handley, P. (1996). *The Creative Trainer*. Cambridge, U.K.: Cambridge University Press.

2. Knoz, A. (1977), quoted by Wlodkowski, R. J. (1999). *Enhancing Adult Motivation to Learn: a comprehensive guide for teaching to all adults*. San Francisco: Jossey-Bass Publishers.

3. Scott, J. "A Time to Learn." *Psychology Today*, 2/10 (1969): 46–48, 66–67, quoted by Wlodkowski, R. J. (1999).

4. Knowles, M. (1984). *The Adult Learner: a neglected species*. Houston: Gulf Publishing Co.

5. Wlodkowski, R. J. (1999).

6. Thorndike, E., quoted by Ormrod, J. (1995). *Human Learning,* 2nd ed. Englewood Cliffs, New Jersey: Merrill.

7. Meyer, L. (1996). *Emotion and Meaning in Music.* Chicago: University of Chicago Press.

8. Thaut, M. "The Influence of Music Therapy Interventions on Self-Rated Changes in Relaxation, Affect, and Thought in Psychiatric Prisoner-Patients." *Journal of Music Therapy,* 26/3 (1989): 155–66.

9. Ehrich, E., and De Bruhl, M. (1996). *The International Thesaurus of Quotations.* New York: HarperCollins Publishers, Inc.

10. Wlodkowski, R. J. (1999).

11. Grout, D., and Palisca, C. (1996). *A History of Western Music,* 5th ed. New York: W.W. Norton & Company.

12. Rogers, C. (1969). *Freedom to Learn.* New York: Macmillan.

13. Herrmann, N. (1989). *The Creative Brain.* Lake Lure, North Carolina: BrainTools, Ned Herrmann Group.

14. Knowles, M. (1984).

15. Wlodkowski, R. J. (1999).

16. Albersnagel, F. "Velten and Musical Mood Induction Procedures: a comparison with accessibility of thought associations." *Behavior Research and Therapy,* 26/1 (1998): 79–86.

17. Borling, J. "The Effect of Seductive Music on Alpha Rhythm and Focused Attention in High-Creative and Low-Creative Subjects." *Journal of Music Therapy,* 18/2 (1981): 101–08.

18. Blood, D., and Feriss, S. "Effects of Background Music on Anxiety, Satisfaction with Communication, and Productivity." *Psychological Reports,* 72/1 (1993): 171–77.

19. Prueter, B., and Mezzano, J. "Effects of Background Music upon Initial Counseling Interaction." *Journal of Music Therapy,* 10 (1973): 205–12.

20. *The 1995 Grolier Multimedia Encyclopedia.* (1995). vr. 7.0.2. Grolier Electronic Publishing, Inc.

21. Morton, L., Kershner, J., and Siegal, L. "The Potential for Therapeutic Applications of Music on Problems Related to Memory and Attention." *Journal of Music Therapy,* 27/4 (1990): 195–208; Thaut, M., and de l'Etoile, S. "The Effects of Music on Mood State-Dependent Recall." *Journal of Music Therapy,* 30/2 (1993): 70–80.

22. Blood, D., and Feriss, S. (1993).

23. Schopenhauer, A. (1966). *The World as Will and Representation,* Volume I. New York: Dover.

24. Lozanov, G. (1978); Lawlor, M., and Handley, P. (1996).

25. Henry, S., and Swartz, R. "Enhancing Healthcare Education with Accelerated Learning Techniques." *Journal of Nursing Staff Development,* 11/1 (1995): 21–24; Hoffman, J., Summers, S., Neff, J., Hanson, S., and Pierce, K. "The Effects of 60 Beats per Minute Music on Test Taking Anxiety among Nursing Students." *Journal of Nursing Education,* 29/2 (1990): 66–70.

26. Wlodkowski, R. J. (1999).

27. Kratus, J., reported in *MuSICA Research Notes,* 2/1 (Spring 1995): <www.musica.uci.edu>.

28. Miles, E. (1997). *Tune Your Brain: using music to manage your mind, body, and mood.* New York: Berkley Books.

29. Adaman, J., and Blaney, P. "The Effects of Musical Mood Induction on Creativity." *Journal of Creative Behavior,* 29/2 (1995): 95–108.

30. Storr, A. (1992). *Music and the Mind.* New York: Random House, Inc.

31. McKinney, C., and Tims, F. "Differential Effects of Selected Classical Music on the Imagery of High versus Low Imagers: two studies." *Journal of Music Therapy,* 22/1 (1995): 22–45.

32. Wlodkowski, R. J. (1999).

33. Ibid.

34. Wilson, E. (1975). *Sociobiology.* Cambridge, Massachusetts: Harvard University Press.

35. Wlodkowski, R. J. (1999).

Chapter 12

TEACHING WITH LYRICS

Most of *Training with a Beat: The Teaching Power of Music* has focused on instrumental music and its placement in learning activities. We have used music to establish a mood, create an environment, encourage memorization, and assist with creativity. We now turn our attention to songs with lyrics. Using music with lyrics can be challenging, but its potential as a learning tool far outweighs its risks.

We begin with a comparison between instrumental and vocal music. The following figure shows one verse of a song. By looking at the music notation, can you comprehend the song's meaning?

Song Melody

If you don't "read" music, the question seems unfair, but people who read music experience the same difficulty. Without lyrics, it is virtually impossible to know what message a song conveys. You can comprehend the sounds, but not the meaning. Musical notation just does not contain enough information. As Igor Stravinsky said, "Music is, by its very nature, essentially powerless to express anything at all."[1]

Music experts always struggle with this problem. Generations of music lovers have imagined Beethoven writing his famous "Moonlight Sonata, Opus 27, No. 2," while viewing moonbeams shimmering across the water. Some people can capture that vision; others cannot. Beethoven emphatically could not. Ludwig Rellstab is responsible for that imagery, not Beethoven. In a performance review, Rellstab described Beethoven's music as reminding him of "moonlight on a lake."[2] Thus the "Moonlight Sonata" was christened, much to Beethoven's chagrin.

We'll never know exactly what Beethoven intended as he wrote the "Moonlight Sonata." Even if Beethoven explained his thought process note by note, each of us would hear it differently. People project their own thoughts, experiences, and visions on instrumental music. The meaning you attach to a piece of music may parallel, or be diametrically opposed, to the vision of another. In his book *Music and the Mind,* Anthony Storr states: "A listener's response to a particular piece of music is governed by his subjective state of mind at the time; and some part of his experiences is likely to be derived from the projection of his own emotions rather than being solely a direct consequence of the music."[3]

You might think this would make placement of music for learning difficult. Fortunately, it does not. As we discovered in our exploration of Emotional Intelligence, people do attach similar emotions to specific pieces of music. According to Wagner, "What music expresses, is eternal, infinite and ideal; it does not express the passion, love, or longing of such-and-such an individual on such-and-such an occasion, but passion, love or longing in itself."[4]

Schopenhauer agrees, stating that music "does not express this or that particular or definite joy, this or that sorrow, or pain, or horror, or delight, or merriment, or peace of mind; but joy, sorrow, pain, horror, delight, merriment, peace of mind themselves."[5]

For teachers, this suggests instrumental music is best used in situations where you intend to establish a generalized mood. If you want to use music for more specific purposes, songs with lyrics become necessary.

Music Note 28

Music with and without lyrics affects people differently:
♪ When people hear music without lyrics, they add their own meaning. Use this music in situations where the music is background to the learning.
♪ When people hear music with lyrics, they may accept your meaning. Use this music in situations where the music is central to the learning.

SONG WITH LYRICS

"The difference between the blues and the blahs is that you can't sing the blahs,"[6] says George Carlin, but you can sing a lyric. The *American Heritage Dictionary* defines "lyric" as "of or relating to a category of poetry that expresses subjective thoughts and feelings, often in a song-like style or form." For our purposes, we will define lyrics as *any verbal or written language that accompanies tonal elements.* With that definition in mind, look again at our example, this time stated as both melody and lyrics.

Song Melody, with Lyrics

The other night dear as I lay sleeping, I dreamt I held you

in my arms. When I a- woke dear I was mis-

-ta - ken, so I hung my head and I cried.

Did the lyrics help you comprehend the song's meaning? Probably so. The lyrics are verbal hints that lead to understanding. Words help define the song's context, telling us what we should feel. When a singer crones "You Are My Sunshine," we can intelligently assume that the song is relationship based, with one person missing the other so desperately that a dream reduces that person to tears. Lyrics allow learners to more readily agree to the specific meaning a song conveys.

REASONS TO USE SONGS WITH LYRICS

Songs with lyrics have several distinct advantages when placed in situations central to the learning. Use songs with lyrics because:

- Songs with lyrics are familiar.
- Words add meaning and depth.
- Singing aids in memorization.

- You can change the lyrics to suit your needs.
- People may walk out of your session singing.

Songs with Lyrics Are Familiar

Symphony concerts usually include compositions by Bach, Mozart, and Beethoven. You might think these works get performed because of their excellence and the sheer number of compositions available. Among these three prolific composers, there are over one thousand compositions worthy of performance. But other composers who have written reams of excellent material have difficulty getting their works heard. Unfortunately for these composers, people want to hear the Bach, Mozart, and Beethoven selections they are familiar with.

Performing musicians know this all too well. Audiences require them to perform the same songs, over and over and over. Many times during my performing career we would learn a song only to put it aside. People had not heard it before and would not accept it. Three weeks later that very same song would hit the radio play lists. The audience would then demand to hear it, sometimes as often as once an hour.

Even famous musicians share this experience. People have little patience with unfamiliar material, making it difficult for the artist to promote their newest release. Artists intentionally sandwich new selections in between the classics, or perform the new releases first, requiring the audience to sit through that material before being rewarded with the music they really want to hear. If, at a popular music concert, you want to conduct your own informal verification survey, pay attention to the order in which songs are performed, and watch the audience's reaction to those selections. The known selections will be positioned to support newer material and will receive more attention and applause, while the rest room lines will grow longer during the performance of new material.

Familiar works are popular precisely because people have heard them before. A familiar song is as comfortable as your worn blue jeans or favorite ice cream. Malcolm Knowles wrote that adults have an accumulated reservoir of experiences that serve as a resource for learning.

Familiar songs draw on those experiences. Knowles also believed that setting the correct learning climate is of critical importance to learning and that the learner has to be ready to learn.[7] Concert halls, ballrooms, parties, and, yes, the classroom can be uncomfortable environments. When people hear a song they have listened to in the privacy of their home, they relax. Comfortable music emotionally warms the training room, placing learners in a receptive frame of mind for learning. Songs with lyrics, especially popular hits of the last fifty years, are extremely useful for this reason. They are old, well-worn, welcome friends.

Words Add Meaning and Depth

Every song lyric tells a story. Margaret Parkin, in her book *Tales for Trainers* remarks, "The power of storytelling lies in the fact that in listening to the content, our conscious mind is occupied, leaving our unconscious mind open to directly receive the underlying message or moral."[8] Song lyrics, when used in this fashion, become metaphors. They place the subject to be taught in the context of the learners' prior experiences. Parkin adds, "Metaphorical language can be much more powerful and can have a more dramatic effect on the listener than literal language."[9]

Author and researcher Michael J. Apter credits this effect to parapathic emotions:

> Parapathic emotions are strong feelings people undergo as they experience something essentially make-believe. People tend to become interested in anything that can induce such emotions. Adults cannot easily turn their attention away from anything that has made them feel deeply. Whenever we use such devices within the context of our learning activities, we will have an excellent means to arouse and sustain learner interest.[10]

Metaphorical song lyrics can serve as vehicles for introduction, discussion, or closure of any training event. For example, during a session on diversity, Randy Newman's song "Short People" could be placed in any of the three contexts.

As an introduction. Play "Short People" as people enter the room. Once the song is over and everyone is seated, call attention to the song's lyrics and ask for comments about the meaning conveyed by those lyrics. Use those comments as a transition to your presentation.

As a discussion point. After presenting your information, ask your learners to read the lyrics and evaluate them in light of what they just learned.

As a closer. Conclude your session by stating, "We are all short people in someone's eyes." Ask the rhetorical question: "If none of us were welcome around here, who would be left to complete our work?" Start the song, thank everyone for attending, and leave the platform. (You will, of course, want to greet everyone at the exit.) Your learners will walk out of the classroom with the song and its lyrics firmly implanted in their brains, and you will have closed with a visually powerful learning point.

Singing Aids in Memorization

If language came from music, as research indicates, it is logical to assume that music with lyrics reaches to the core of our being. It certainly has been proven true that words synchronized with music are easy to learn. You experienced this if you completed the lyrical learning table in chapter 7. It appears that this technique is effective regardless of intellectual ability. Even children with severely limited mental capacity can recall material when taught in a song.[11]

Language is, as we saw in our discussion of the brain's left and right hemispheres, predominately processed in the left hemisphere, and harmony is comprehended in the right. Lyrics engage both the lyrically focused left hemisphere and the melodically focused right hemisphere. For centuries, children the world over have learned their lessons in song. Unfortunately, adults forget the usefulness of this technique.

You Can Change the Lyrics to Suit Your Needs

Any concept can be taught with lyrics. Simply rewrite a song's lyrics to reflect your key lesson points and have your learners sing along. Vocal ability is not important. What matters is engaging both sides of your learners' brains. The verse below offers a simple example. The lyrics of the well-known children's song "Mary Had a Little Lamb" have been rewritten to reflect one of our key learning points.

Songs that teach are learning tools, learning tools, learning tools,
Songs that teach are learning tools, when people sing along.
Music teaches everyone, everyone, everyone,
Music teaches everyone, the learning's in the song.

By having your trainees sing a song with your lyrics, you will increase their chances of remembering the material as their minds replay your lyrics over and over.

People May Walk out of Your Session Singing

Music sticks in your learners' brains. They may sing the learning to themselves for days, remembering your capable instruction and reviewing key concepts in song. Besides, when was the last time people left your classroom singing?

Music Note 29

Use songs with lyrics because:
♪ Songs with lyrics are familiar.
♪ Words add meaning and depth.
♪ Singing aids in memorization.
♪ You can change the lyrics to suit your needs.
♪ People may walk out of your session singing.

DIFFICULTIES PRESENTED BY SONGS WITH LYRICS

Songs with lyrics are not risk free. There are several difficulties associated with their use:

- Lyrics can trigger personal memories.
- Some lyrics have hidden meaning.
- Lyrics can make concentration difficult.
- Language barriers may become a factor.

Lyrics Can Trigger Personal Memories

Popular songs are teeming with personal memories. If one of your learners starts crying because their cat died while "that song" was playing, it could destroy the classroom environment. Unfortunately, there is no way of knowing in advance when one of your learners will have an emotional reaction to a specific song. To minimize potential repercussions, make intelligent decisions about the material you use. If the context you have placed the song in is appropriate and meaningful, these kind of situations are less likely to occur.

Some Lyrics Have Hidden Meaning

Often we enjoy a song without knowing its meaning. The mood of a song can be so inviting that the intent of the lyrics gets ignored. One example is the Los del Rio song "Macarena." The dance inspired by that song became wildly popular in the 1990s. At the 1996 Democratic Party nominating convention, U.S. Vice President Al Gore made humorous comments about his ability to "do the Macarena." Unfortunately, none of his advisers had researched the song's lyrics. If they had, they would have discovered a song about a woman who cheats on her boyfriend one night with his two best friends. Certainly, this is not the kind of message the vice president intended to convey.

Lyrics can also take on cultural meanings far removed from the original context. Many composers find the public misinterpreting their work in different, unexpected ways. One such example is the Beatles song "Yellow Submarine." Paul McCartney describes the song's creation as follows:

I was lying in bed in this little limbo-land just before you slip into sleep. I remember thinking that a children's song would be quite a good idea and I thought of images, and the colour yellow came to me, and a submarine came to me, and I thought, that's kind of nice, like a toy, very childish yellow submarine. I just made up a little tune in my head, then started making a story, sort of an ancient mariner, telling the young kids where he'd lived and how there'd been a place where he had a yellow submarine.[12]

Note the childlike innocence of McCartney's description, how idyllic his vision was. In spite of this intent, "Yellow Submarine" became a major psychedelic trip for 1960s drug culture contemporaries.

These comments should not be read as a criticism of "Macarena" or "Yellow Submarine." It is rather a demonstration that you must learn all you can about a song before you use it. Someone in your class might know a song's intended, or implied, meaning. You want the songs you choose to reinforce your teachings, not distract with unwelcome or surprising messages.

Lyrics Can Make Concentration Difficult

If a song is too popular, people may start singing the lyrics, or they may pay attention to the song instead of you. In addition, introverts remember significantly less than extroverts when learning while pop music radio is playing in the background.[13] This difficulty can be overcome by playing songs with lyrics in situations where you plan to draw attention to the music. If your learners then decide to sing along, you will receive credit for your clever instructional design.

Language Barriers May Become a Factor

The story in the song, and any metaphors that can be drawn from it, will not matter if your song is in a language different from the one spoken by your learners. In this situation, the music becomes background to the learning. To be effective, lyrics must communicate in the learner's language.

Music Note 30

> *When using songs with lyrics, watch for potential dangers:*
> ♪ *Lyrics can trigger personal memories.*
> ♪ *Some lyrics have hidden meaning.*
> ♪ *Lyrics can make concentration difficult.*
> ♪ *Language barriers may become a factor.*

Now that we have considered the difficulties songs with lyrics present, we will broaden our focus to include the risks involved in using any sort of music for learning. Several potential challenges must be recognized. In the next chapter, we will consider those challenges and explore ways to overcome them.

Notes

1. Stravinsky, I. (1975). *Igor Stravinsky, an Autobiography*. London, U.K.: Calder and Boyers.

2. Reported by Storr, A. (1992). *Music and the Mind*. New York: Random House, Inc.

3. Ibid.

4. Wagner, quoted by Langer, S. (1960). *Philosophy in a New Key*. Cambridge, Massachusetts: Harvard University Press.

5. Schopenhauer, A. (1883). *The World as Will and Idea*. Haldane, R. B., and Kemp, J., eds. vol. 1. London, U.K.: Trubner.

6. Carlin, G. (1997). *Brain Droppings*. New York: Hyperion.

7. Knowles, M. (1984). *The Adult Learner: a neglected species*. Houston: Gulf Publishing Co.

8. Parkin, M. (1998). *Tales for Trainers*. Sterling, Virginia: Stylus Publishing.

9. Ibid.

10. Wlodkowski, R. J. (1999). *Enhancing Adult Motivation to Learn: a comprehensive guide for teaching to all adults*. San Francisco: Jossey-Bass Publishers.

11. Farnsworth, P. (1969). *The Social Psychology of Music*. Iowa: Iowa State University Press.

12. Miles, B. (1997). *Paul McCartney: many years from now*. New York: Henry Holt and Company.

13. Furnham, A., and Bradley, A. "Music while You Work: the differential distraction of background music on the cognitive test performance of introverts and extroverts." *Applied Cognitive Psychology*, 11 (1997): 445–55.

Chapter 13

MUSICAL PRECAUTIONS

Illustration by J. Chuck Johnson

The Blues

"STOP PLAYING MUSIC," he shouted urgently, *"RIGHT NOW."*

He did not consider what we played to be music, so I was not sure what to stop. When we had arrived, he told me his patrons liked two kinds of music. *"They like country good enough."*

"We're not a country act," I thought. It was always a problem for traveling musical groups like mine. We had just finished a highly successful engagement at the Sonesta Key Biscayne, Florida. That crowd

had wanted to hear the same music the rest of the country was listening to, and we knew the songs. Our next performance of any real consequence was in Midland, Texas, quite a drive from Miami. We had three weeks to get there, so we booked one-week engagements along the line. That way, we could travel toward Texas and still keep the money rolling in. We took this job, en route, at "Robby's Rolling Pig."

Anyhow, the problem for traveling groups was knowing for sure what songs the people in the next location would want to hear. So, I thought to myself, "We can dust off a few of the popular country songs we used to perform, but the people in the club must like other kinds of music too."

Then Robby dropped his other shoe, "And when they're not listening to country music, they like western music."

I smiled, but inside I was thinking sarcastically, "Country AND western. Now, that's variety!"

It wasn't worth changing our entire repertoire to satisfy this one owner for a low-paying, one-week engagement. Besides, we had an act. The music we performed was first class. It was better to be disliked and good than to be disliked and bad. We relearned the country songs we could, and performed them along with our normal repertoire.

Three nights and several arguments later, here was Robby, stopping us while we performed the only song of ours he liked. "STOP PLAYING MUSIC!" he hollered, loud enough to be heard by us over the music. We had, however, stopped by the time he said "MUSIC!" Everyone in the club, including two suited types sitting up front—they were really the only ones paying attention—heard the word.

"Robby, what is it you need from us?" I asked, my patience wearing thin.

"I don't care what you play," he whispered over the top of the piano. "Do your songs, make things up, whatever you want. I'll pay you double the rate for tonight, but no songs anyone's heard before."

I was really confused. In three short, agony-filled days, we had gone from "rework your song list" to "perform originals and make things up."

"If that's what you really want," I said, "We can do that, but what about those two?" I pointed to the two men, almost too interested in our conversation, sitting at the front table, "They're actually listening."

"Show them what writing a song sounds like," he muttered, and stomped off.

"Let's play a blues in A," I directed the musicians, "Does anyone feel like making some lyrics up?"

Of course it was Larry, our group comedian, who volunteered. He donned some shades, approached the mike with an attitude, and his best B. B. King blues singer impersonation voice, sang:

> Ba ba da da.
> This club sure smells bad,
> Ba ba da da.
> It really does reek,
> Ba ba da da.
> I'm glad that we're here,
> Ba ba da da.
> For just one more week!

And the band, all smiles, joined in.

> It's a real pig pen,
> Robby's place is bad news,
> I sure do hate it,
> I've got the Rolling Pig Pen blues.

That night, the band played exceptionally well. Our two fans listened for a while, laughed, and left. Amazing, Robby thanked us for Larry's song, and paid the extra money he had promised.

It was only later that I figured out what had happened. Our two fans were from the American Society of Composers, Authors, and Publishers (ASCAP). Their job was to estimate the amount of copyrighted material performed nightly at Robby's Rolling Pig. From their estimation, a monthly fee for copyrighted material would be charged. Robby had tried to beat the law by not allowing us to perform any published music.

The ASCAP men were not fooled. They charged The Rolling Pig the maximum average their formula would allow. By the time the bill arrived, Robby was the one with the "Rolling Pig Pen Blues."

We have explored potential dangers involving the use of lyrics. There are some other precautions to take when using music. They include:

- ignoring cultural norms
- misreading learner expectations
- technical difficulties
- cost and time considerations
- copyright law

Ignoring Cultural Norms

Music fulfills different needs in diverse locations around the world, and we are all prisoners of our cultural assumptions. Individuals, even professional musicians, have a difficult time appreciating the nuances of music outside their heritage. Erroneous music placement based on mistaken cultural assumptions is a potential source for embarrassment when training with music. You must know the cultural assumptions and expectations of your audience before selecting material.

The musical traditions of Africa, India, and the West demonstrate this contrast. Western music is very focused on structure and form. Listening is an experience unto itself. People use this music to offer commentary, share emotions, and enjoy art for art's sake. African music, with its repeating patterns and ritualistic quality, is often associated with dance. Scholar Leonard Meyer, in his book *Emotion and Meaning in Music*, reports:

> In the West, for example, death is usually depicted by slow tempi and low ranges, while in certain African tribes it is portrayed in frenzied musical activity; yet this results from differences in attitudes toward death rather than from differences in the associative processes of the human mind. The particular way in which a connotation is realized or represented in music cannot be understood apart from the beliefs and attitudes of the culture in question.[1]

In India, ragas are woven into the fabric of life. Each raga represents an individual emotional quality suitable for performance only under certain conditions. The performer, the music, and the listeners must all be on the same mental and emotional plane. If they are not the performance cannot occur.[2]

Communication technologies have spread Western music worldwide. The future trend is a likely continuation of this phenomenon, combined with the assimilation of different cultural styles and musical flavors. Even as musical traditions evolve and merge, individual tastes and assumptions will remain. The effective trainer knows the cultural assumptions of the audience. The teaching power of music only works when you and your trainees share the same beat.

Music Note 31

> Know the cultural assumptions and expectations of your audience.

The following chart offers a comparative example featuring four different musical traditions.

Music Purposes Chart

Culture	Style	Purpose	Instrument
Africa	Repetition, polyphonic sounds, conversation between instruments, dense textures	Transmits knowledge, celebrates occasions, organizes work activities	Percussion instruments, thumb piano, lutes, lyres, harps, and zithers, flutes, whistles, oboes, and trumpets
India	24 tone scales, fixed background pitch, rhythmic cycle of a fixed number of beats, reoccurring themes, improvisation	Expresses certain moods or emotions, believed to personify gods, ascetics, or devotees	Tambura, drums, sitar, shahnai, sarangivina, the venu, the nagasvaram, and the Western violin
Japan	5 tone scales, music closely allied to verbal expression, minimal instrumentation, emphasis on melodic and rhythmic tension	Story telling, drama, Buddhist chant	Flutes, koto, oboes, mouth organ, zither, lute, drums
Europe and the United States	12 tone scales, extremely organized, major-minor focus, somewhat rhythmic	Express emotions, celebrate occasions, offer commentary	Traditional orchestra instruments, electronic guitars and keyboards

SOURCE: *The 1995 Grolier Multimedia Encyclopedia.* (1995). vr. 7.0.2. Grolier Electronic Publishing, Inc.

Misreading Learner Expectations

A person's relationship to music, as we saw described by Friedrich Nietzsche in chapter 1, is personal, almost lovelike. Meyer states, "Music presents a generic event which then becomes particularized in the experience of the listener."[3] People respond to music on individual terms, according to individual definitions, with solitary visions of past experience. Meyer continues, "A sight, a sound, or a fragrance evokes half-forgotten thoughts of persons, places, and experiences; stirs up dreams 'mixing memory with desire'; or awakens conscious connotations of referential things."[4] You may be able to frame a piece of music's meaning, but it is almost impossible to overcome deeply rooted memories. Meyer offers this example:

> Even where the original association appears to be relevant and appropriate to the character of the music being played, affective experience may be a result of the private meaning which the image has for that particular listener. The image of a triumphal processional might within a given culture be relevant to the character of a piece of music; but the association might for private reasons arouse feelings of humiliation or defeat. Thus while the image itself is relevant to the music, the significance which it has for the particular individual is purely personal.[5]

Raymond Wlodkowski formulated several strategies for enhancing adult-learning motivation. One of those was, "To the degree authentically possible, reflect the language, perspective, and attitudes of your adult learners."[6] Your selection of music will either reflect your learners perceptions, or impede the learning environment. A song may have personal relevance to you, while not being appropriate for your trainees' needs. Poorly selected music can distract people in situations where concentration is critical.[7] You cannot, and should not, ignore your personal taste in music. Nevertheless, select musical material that paces and mirrors your learners and that is within their realm of experience.[8]

Music Note 32

Select music that paces and mirrors your learners.

Technical Difficulties

Music requires sound projection equipment. Considering that a typical trainer's technological requirements may already include a TV/VCR setup, a laptop computer, an overhead projector, and other miscellaneous training materials, class setup and facilitation become time-consuming and complicated. If the audio system fails, can your training still succeed?

The best approach for mastering technology is simplicity. Use the most common technology available, and create a fallback plan for every conceivable scenario. If you are using CDs, carry a backup audiocassette, or record the material on a VHS tape. For my music presentations, I arrive with a complete presentation software packet, an audiocassette and a duplicate back-up, the original CDs, and time code listings for all these items. I also bring my own portable CD-cassette player in case of an unforseen technical prob-  lem with the location's audio system. If technical problems occur with the presentation software, I have given myself plenty of options from which to choose. After all, music samples are a major expectation of any presentation about music. Technical problems cannot control those who are prepared for them.

Music Note 33

Be prepared for any technical problems that may occur.

Cost and Time Considerations

The selection of appropriate music requires familiarity with the musical repertoire available. A trainer must purchase CDs or cassettes, listen to the material, catalog different selections for different uses, and follow current musical trends, purchasing new material as it becomes available. The whole enterprise can be expensive and time-consuming. "Greatest hits" and "compilation" albums are excellent resources for keeping costs low while quickly building a collection of an artist's, or genre's, best works.

Music Note 34

Purchase greatest hits and compilation collections.

There are some excellent collections of music for different moods. Mood-inducing music compact disks are perhaps the ideal trainer's resource. They offer a consistency of mood from one selection to the next, allowing you to play any cut on the album with confidence, knowing that the mood, volume level, and emotion of the music will remain constant throughout the album. Specific recommendations are offered in the appendices.

Music-purchasing clubs are another trainer's resource. Most of these clubs offer free CDs or cassettes in exchange for additional purchases. You can build a collection quickly, remain current by reading the purchasing club's monthly flyer, and cancel when your collection is complete enough to meet your needs. An added bonus, in the case of musical trainers, is that the materials you purchase may be tax deductible.

Music Note 35

Join a music club.

Copyright Law

Music, just like real estate, is owned. Whereas real estate is tangible, music is considered "intellectual" property, providing the creator, or the person who the creator sells the work to, with all the rights and considerations that any owner can claim, including the right to sell or rent the property. Penalties for ignoring copyright law can be quite severe. This book is not intended to, and does not, constitute legal advice. It only provides illustrative and descriptive information on general legal concepts. Before you decide to use another person's legally copyrighted material, obtain the advice of legal counsel.

Music Note 36

> Before using copyrighted music, obtain the advice of legal counsel.

Within the context of a generic overview, there are three general legal concepts to understand. They are:

- public domain
- copyright protection
- fair use

Public Domain

Musical compositions "in the public domain" are not protected by copyright law. Most of the music composed before the last century falls into this category and can be used free of charge by anyone. Specific compilations of works, or performances, can, however, be copyrighted.

Music Note 37

> Songs in the public domain can be performed by anyone.

Copyright Protection

With regard to music, a copyright is a form of protection provided by law to the musical composition's owner. Copyright protects the owner from unauthorized use, thereby providing the owner with the right to decide who can "copy" the work.

Music Note 38

> A copyright owner controls who can "copy" the music.

Every country has its own copyright law, but most countries offer protection to foreign works under certain conditions and follow some standard practices as agreed to under the Berne Convention and other international treaty agreements. The information contained in *Training with a Beat* is contained in Title 17 of the United States Code. This book is not intended to, and does not, constitute legal advice. It only provides illustrative and descriptive information on general legal concepts. For more accurate and up-to-date information, you should refer to the laws of the country in which you conduct your training.

According to Title 17 of the United States Code, copyrights usually last for life plus a period of years (usually varying between fifty and seventy years) after the death of the author. Any unauthorized use can be cause for imprisonment or substantial fines or both. Every time you play a CD, sing "Happy Birthday," make a copy of a tape, or play a recording for other people without paying royalties, you could be in violation of copyright law.

Copyright owners have joined together to protect their interests by joining organizations that collect royalties for song usages. A music-performing rights organization represents songwriters; film, television, musical theater, and classical music composers; and music publishers. Typically, performing rights organizations collect royalties from businesses that use that music in the course of their daily activities. The organization then distributes that money to the composers and publishers of the musical works. Some of the primary organizations are listed in the "Other Music Resources" appendices section. Two of the best known are the American Society of Composers, Authors, and Publishers (ASCAP) and Broadcast Music Inc. (BMI). These organizations work under a fee arrangement in which establishments pay an averaged fee in exchange for blanket protection from prosecution.

Fair Use

The intent of copyright law is to protect the owner while still allowing for appropriate usage of the work. U.S. copyright law contains a provision called "fair use." If the usage is a "fair use," the copyright owner may not have to be notified of, or grant permission for, the usage.

Music Note 39

> If the usage is a "fair use," the copyright owner may not have to be notified of, or grant permission for, the usage.

Fortunately for the musical trainer, a number of fair use restrictions exist as related to:

- performances
- recordings
- transmissions

Performances. A performance may be considered legal if the performance is:

- by instructors or pupils in the face-to-face teaching activities of a nonprofit educational institution, in a classroom or similar place devoted to instruction
- performed in the course of services at a place of worship or other religious assembly
- without any purpose of direct or indirect commercial advantage and without payment of any fee or other compensation for the performance to any of its performers, promoters, or organizers (1) if there is no direct or indirect admission charge or (2) if the proceeds, after deducting the reasonable costs of producing the performance, are used exclusively for

educational, religious, or charitable purposes and not for private financial gain

- by a governmental body or a nonprofit agricultural or horticultural organization

- during a social function organized and promoted by a non-profit veterans or fraternal organization to which the general public is not invited if the proceeds from the performance, after deducting the reasonable costs of producing the performance, are used exclusively for charitable purposes and not for financial gain

Reproduction. Reproduction for criticism, comment, news reporting, teaching scholarship, and research may not constitute a violation. You should always seek legal advice if you are unclear of the law in your country. Some factors that should be considered permissible include:

- whether the use is of a commercial nature or is for nonprofit educational purposes. If a profit is being made, the reproduction may constitute a violation of law.

- the amount and substantiality of the portion used in relation to the copyrighted work as a whole. If you just use a small amount of the piece of music, in some cases, you may not be in violation of copyright law.

- the effect of the use on the potential market for or value of the copyrighted work. Generally speaking, if your usage deprives the song owner of monies that person would otherwise have earned, you are in violation.

Transmissions. A transmission is sometimes considered a "fair use," if the transmission is:

- specifically designed for and primarily directed to blind or other handicapped persons who are unable to read normal printed material as a result of their handicap

- a regular part of the instructional activities of a governmental body or a nonprofit educational institution and the performance is directly related to the teaching content of the transmission

Some businesses may be able to transmit audiotapes and CDs within their business establishment if the transmission is:

- confined within the business establishment
- for use in the ordinary course of business
- on a single receiving apparatus of a kind commonly used in private homes, unless a direct charge is made to see or hear the transmission; or the transmission is further transmitted to the public
- no advance program listing the specific sound recordings transmitted

If you choose to transmit musical compositions in this manner, seek legal counsel to ensure your legal protection.

Finally, there are some general questions you should consider before using copyrighted material. Is the usage:

- For profit? If the intent of the training is to improve job performance for a business, your usage may not be a fair use.
- For charity? Charity events are exempt from royalty collection.
- Being presented without direct charge? Music used in an incidental fashion, without charge for its performance, may be legal.
- Without commercial advantage? If there is a profit being made from the usage, royalties are probably due.
- Being transmitted on a single receiving apparatus of a kind commonly used in private homes with no additional transmission to the public? Single transmitting devices do not usually constitute public address systems, and as such, are not usually considered a broadcasting of the material.

- Affecting the market potential of the copyrighted work? If your usage supplants the normal market, it likely is an infringement.

- Published in an advance program? The trainer who publishes an advance listing of musical selections to be performed may be both supplanting the market potential of the work by encouraging people to attend the session because of the music to be presented and indicating an intention to violate copyright law.

This book is not intended to, and does not, provide legal advice. It is critical to obtain legal advice if you use copyrighted material. Many national governments provide copyright information on request. To request copyright information, simply contact your national government entity for information relating to the laws in your country.

Finally, trainers who respect music never use musical material without crediting the composer and performer of the work. This is not to suggest that you should interrupt your session to draw attention to the background music. Rather, it is a recommendation of professional courtesy whenever and wherever possible. The music exists because a composer was willing to share deep-felt emotions with the rest of humanity. The usage of such inspiration deserves professional respect and recognition.

Notes

1. Meyer, L. B. (1956). *Emotion and Meaning in Music*. Chicago: Chicago Press.

2. *The 1995 Grolier Multimedia Encyclopedia*. (1995). vr. 7.0.2. Grolier Electronic Publishing, Inc.

3. Meyer, L. B. (1956).

4. Ibid.

5. Ibid.

6. Wlodkowski, R. J. (1999). *Enhancing Adult Motivation to Learn: a comprehensive guide for teaching to all adults*. San Francisco: Jossey-Bass Publishers.

7. *The 1995 Grolier Multimedia Encyclopedia.* (1995).

8. Wlodkowski, R. J. (1999).

CHAPTER 14

TRAINING WITH A BEAT

(W)e have discussed a wide variety of information during *Training with a Beat: The Teaching Power of Music*, exploring everything from the birth of music to its usage in the modern world. Along the way, we have:

- seen numerous examples of effective music placement within the learning environment

- discovered that music can move our emotions, inspire us to action, heal our mind and body, encourage active dreaming, and create new ideas within us

- explored various theories that may explain the teaching power of music

- seen examples of musical placement within the learning environment

But, why does music work as a learning tool? Music is an ever present force in our lives, and yet it is usually on the margins of our consciousness. How can something so subliminal contain so much power?

The answer may lie in life's margins. As Sir Arthur Conan Doyle wrote in *The Adventures of Sherlock Holmes,* "It has long been an axiom of mine that the little things are infinitely the most important."[1]

I believe that success in life is all about the margin. Massive change is difficult, if not impossible to create. Life moves slowly, at its own pulse. All social entities, cultures, governments, and organizations build up traditions, history, and mores that provide the rules for daily existence. To truly change one of these entities would be difficult, if not impossible.

Fortunately, it is not necessary to completely remake an entity. It is only necessary to change it at the margins:

- When discussing politics, people often complain that the different candidates are more alike than they are different. Although it is true that the candidates are alike in many ways, great issues are usually involved in elections, and it is in the small margins of the candidates' differences where most policy changes occur.

- In sports, the difference between winning and losing is often not a difference between 50 percent and 100 percent effort. The difference is usually minuscule, perhaps one or two percentage points. Certainly final game scores demonstrate this fact. Often the winner is not the team or individual scoring twenty more points. Sometimes one point separates the winner from the loser.

People are overloaded with stimuli. Conversations, information, traffic, people, and machinery bombard people all day. It makes a mind weary.

Businesses pay advertisers millions of dollars to reach through this clutter. The commercial you half watch as you fix a snack during a television show break cost millions of dollars. Businesses do not pay for your undivided attention. They pay for access to the margins of your attention.

So it is with learning. People have their own learning preferences. No amount of teacher effort alters that fact. Learners may ignore your lecture, your discussion, or your activities. They may be thinking about last night's date, tonight's concert, tomorrow's important meeting. Their focus will never match your own. Effective learning takes place where music lives—in the margins.

It is true that music will never substitute for a solid teaching experience. It is not a replacement for effective lecturing, nor is it the only resource available. Rather, music is one more tool effective trainers should have at their disposal. Music, by its very familiarity, does not draw attention to itself. Instead, it works much as coffee comforts the morning, popcorn anticipates the movie, and baking bread remembers home; it awakens the recesses of your learners' minds, it calls the emotion to attention, it opens up the margin, by paralleling the pulse of everyday life. For life has a rhythm, music has a meter, and training, if done properly, has a beat.

Music Note 40

Training, if done properly, has a beat.

Note

1. Doyle, A., quoted in *Webster's Dictionary of Quotations*. (1995). New York: Smithmark Publishers.

Appendices

1. **Resources Introduction**
2. **Music Notes**
3. **Glossary**
4. **Classical Music Resources**
5. **Other Music Resources**
6. **Pop Placement by Song**
7. **Pop Placement by Artist**
8. **Pop Placement by Function**
9. **Music Placement Matrix**

It's not the notes that make the music.
It's the meaning behind the notes.

—Roger Benedict

1. Resources Introduction

The resources that constitute the next several pages are provided to help you transfer the learning contained within this book to your own environment:

- The "Music Notes" section, summarizing key learning points throughout the book, will help you ensure that your musical usage is appropriate and effective.

- The glossary is a useful tool for comprehending the meaning of words and phrases, especially the musical terms, referenced throughout the book.

- The "Classical Music Resources" and "Other Music Resources" listings recommend ways in which you can begin building your own music library.

- The three different "Pop Placement" listings, cross-referenced by artist, song title, and learning function, offer a comprehensive listing of popular music selections from the last fifty years and suggest appropriate popular song placement in several learning environments.

- The music placement matrix offers a method for matching different types and styles of music to specific situations.

- The index will help you quickly find details relating to specific information contained within the book.

These resources will aid your instructional design, facilitation, and teaching endeavors. They will increase your ability to effectively apply your musical beat in any learning situation.

2. Music Notes

Music Note   1: Music has numerous effects on people:
- Music affects shopping habits.
- Music affects mood.
- Music affects productivity.
- Music affects health.

Music Note   2: Music may be the original language.

Music Note   3: Music may have begun as a way of:
- communicating with God
- joining together
- attracting a mate
- expressing love
- communicating between adults and infants

Music Note   4: If trainees are having emotionally pleasant experiences in your classroom, their learning may increase.

Music Note   5: The human brain has three layers. Each hears music in its own way:
- The reptilian brain hears sound as vibration.
- The limbic system hears sound as feeling.
- The neocortex hears sound intellectually.

Music Note   6: Music appeals to both the left and right hemispheres:
- The left hemisphere processes rhythm and lyrics.
- The right hemisphere listens for melodies and harmonic relationships across time.

Music Note   7: Children who study music become effective adult learners.

2. Music Notes ♪

Music Note   8: Alpha brain waves encourage reflection. Use slow, minor-key music to foster Alpha waves.

Beta brain waves wake the brain up, making it more alert. Use fast, major-key music to encourage Beta waves.

Music Note   9: Music is a core learning intelligence.

Music Note 10: Music reaches people's intelligence:
- helping people feel engaged and competent
- providing a multidimensional view of learning topics
- breaking through a trainee's wall of resistance
- touching people's emotions, reaching a deeper level of understanding and communication

Music Note 11: Children learn by singing. Adults should too.

Music Note 12: Music is organized sound.

Music Note 13: The two primary elements of music are rhythm and melody.

Music Note 14: A time period signifies the number of beats per time period over the kind of note that receives a beat.

Music Note 15: The two primary time signatures are $\frac{4}{4}$ and $\frac{3}{4}$.

Music Note 16: Select training music you can walk or sway to.

Music Note 17: Air molecules plus vibrations create sound.

Music Note 18: Audio frequencies affect humans:
- High-frequency sounds affect cognitive functions.
- Middle-frequency sounds stimulate the heart, lungs, and the emotions.
- Low-frequency sounds affect physical movement.

2. Music Notes ♪ ♪ ♪ ♪ ♪ ♪ ♪ ♪ ♪ ♪ ♪ ♪ ♪ ♪ ♪ ♪(continued)

Music Note 19: Most Western music divides the octave into twelve notes.

Music Note 20: It is the relationship between sounds we hear as music.

Music Note 21: Major keys sound happy; minor keys sound sad:
- Major-key music cools the brain, encouraging better moods.
- Minor-key music warms the brain, making it more alert.

Music Note 22: Use different types of music for different needs:
- Vivaldi, Bach, Mozart, and early Beethoven are ideal for most learning situations.
- Use sound track songs in situations where the song addresses your specific training matter.
- Use movie sound track instrumentals to match specific moods.
- Use pop music that is at least ten years old.
- Use jazz in situations where the music is intentionally highlighted.
- Use New Age music in dreamy brainstorming situations.

Music Note 23: The best songs are those that have both clarity of form and purpose.

Music Note 24: Following the "Mozart Music Meter," training music should:
- maintain a constant tempo
- maintain a constant volume level
- feature consistent instrumentation
- not draw attention to itself

2. Music Notes ♪

Music Note 25: Music with a beat helps trainees:

- repeat monotonous tasks with a higher level of interest
- work longer and faster
- focus on the task at hand
- build consistency and increase speed

Music Note 26: Use the tempo of the music to change energy levels:

- High-rhythmic activity in $\frac{3}{4}$ excites people.
- Low-rhythmic activity in $\frac{4}{4}$ calms people.
- Fast, major-key music encourages better learning moods.
- Slow music helps people relax.

Music Note 27: Music can be used to:

- establish a positive learning environment
- minimize negative conditions surrounding a subject
- create a metaphor for the task to be learned
- provide background sound
- assist with repeated tasks
- aid memorization
- transport your learners to different times and locales
- enhance reviews
- frame games and activities
- change energy levels
- foster creativity
- provide closure

2. Music Notes ♪ ♪ ♪ ♪ ♪ ♪ ♪ ♪ ♪ ♪ ♪ ♪ ♪ ♪ ♪(continued)

Music Note 28: Music with and without lyrics affects people differently:

- When people hear music without lyrics, they add their own meaning. Use this music in situations where the music is background to the learning.
- When people hear music with lyrics, they may accept your meaning. Use this music in situations where the music is central to the learning.

Music Note 29: Use songs with lyrics because:

- Songs with lyrics are familiar.
- Words add meaning and depth.
- Singing aids in memorization.
- You can change the lyrics to suit your needs.
- People may walk out of your session singing.

Music Note 30: When using songs with lyrics, watch for potential dangers:

- Lyrics can trigger personal memories.
- Some lyrics have hidden meaning.
- Lyrics can make concentration difficult.
- Language barriers may become a factor.

Music Note 31: Know the cultural assumptions and expectations of your audience.

Music Note 32: Select music that paces and mirrors your learners.

Music Note 33: Be prepared for any technical problem that could occur.

Music Note 34: Purchase greatest hits and compilation collections.

Music Note 35: Join a music club.

Music Note 36: Before using copyrighted music, obtain the advice of legal counsel.

2. Music Notes ♪

Music Note 37: Songs in the public domain can be performed by anyone.

Music Note 38: A copyright owner controls who can "copy" the music.

Music Note 39: If the usage is a "fair use," the copyright owner may not have to be notified of, or grant permission for, the usage.

Music Note 40: Training, if done properly, has a beat.

3. Glossary of Musical Terms and Definitions

Active concert:
A dynamic recitation of learning material to the accompaniment of classical music, created by Dr. Georgi Lozanov

Alpha waves:
The brain's waves (around 8 to 13 cycles per second) when in a nonaroused, relaxed state of awareness

Beta waves:
The brain's waves (around 13 to 30 cycles per second) of an awake, conscious mind

Classical music:
The historical cultural music of the Western civilization, begun in Greece and spread by the Roman Empire

Copyright:
A form of protection provided by law to a piece of music's owner, granting the right to decide who can "copy" the work

Corpus callosum:
The connecting nerve tissue between the left and right hemispheres of the brain

Delta waves:
The brain's waves (around 1 to 4 cycles) when in a deep, dreamless sleep

Emotional Intelligence:
Daniel Goleman's theory that people need the emotive limbic system skills, and that being in touch with those emotions leads to success

Equal temperament:
A music intonation system by which all the notes between an octave are arbitrarily and equally divided with a frequency ratio of 1.05946 between each tone

Fair use:
Exceptions in the copyright law that allow for public usage of copyrighted material without royalty fees

3. Glossary of Musical Terms and Definitions ♪ ♪ ♪ ♪ ♪

Intonation: The sounding relationship between simultaneously vibrating notes

Left hemisphere: The predominately logical and analytical side of the brain, hearing music sequentially, focusing on rhythm and lyrics

Limbic system: The emotional center of the brain, controlling hormones, thirst, hunger, sexuality, the body's pleasure centers, metabolism, the autonomic nervous system, portions of long-term memory, and tasked with feeling the emotion in music

Lyrics: Any verbal or written language that accompanies tonal elements

Major keys: Scales that have a happy feeling, creating positive-sounding music useful for rock and marches

Manuscript: A document that records the sounds and rhythms contained within a piece of music

Measure: A time period indicating the basic pulse of a piece of music

Melody: A series of tones that, when sounded together, create a pleasurable listening experience

Minor keys: Scales that have a sad feeling, giving music a reflective sound ideal for waltzes, classical music, and pop ballad

Multiple Intelligences: Howard Gardner's theory that eight core intelligences are present to some degree within every individual. One of the core intelligences is music/rhythmic.

3. Glossary of Musical Terms and Definitions ♪ ♪(continued)

Music:
An aesthetically pleasing or harmonious sound or combination of sounds, from the Greek word *mousikos,* meaning "of the muses"

Neocortex:
The brain's center of logic, absorbing sounds and organizing them into a coherent whole

Notation:
The creation of arbitrary representations for each tone sounded in a piece of music, including a series of bars and spaces naming different tones and their relationship to each other

Octave:
The tones that result when a frequency is doubled or halved

Passive concert:
A reflective recitation of learning material to the accompaniment of classical music, created by Dr. Georgi Lozanov

Reptilian brain:
The portion of the brain that emerges out of the spinal column, driven by instinct. It controls breathing, pulse, heart rate, and instincts, and sorts incoming sounds

Right hemisphere:
The holistic and metaphorical side of the brain, sorting the continuously evolving relationships and situations of music, including the performance of different instruments, sounds, dynamics, harmonies over time, and melodies

Royalty fees:
The fees that must be paid to the owner of a piece of music in exchange for the usage of that work

Scales:
The division of the frequencies between an octave into a series of tones

3. Glossary of Musical Terms and Definitions ♪ ♪ ♪ ♪ ♪

Sound:

The tones that result when air molecules vibrate

Theta waves:

The brain's waves (around 4 to 8 cycles per second) in the shallow stages of sleep, or in deep contemplation, or meditation

Time signature:

An agreed on representation of how many sounds will be performed within a specific time period

Triune brain:

Dr. Paul MacLean's theory of brain development in three stages: reptilian, limbic (Paleomammalian), and neocortex (Neomammalian)

4. Classical Music Resources

Set Your Life to Music Series

The Phillips "Set Your Life to Music" series could have been designed specifically for trainers; it is that good. The beauty of the series lies in the way each CD is tailor-made for specific activities, as labeled on the CDs. This programming allows a trainer to play any track on the selected CD with the assurance that the music will maintain a consistency of volume, tempo, and mood. In addition, the CD titles simplify the process of selecting music appropriate for each learning activity.

Titles:
  "Bach at Bedtime"
  "Bach for Book Lovers"
  "Bach for Breakfast"
  "Beethoven at Bedtime"
  "Beethoven for Beloved"
  "Debussy at Dawn"
  "Debussy for Daydreaming"
  "Mozart at Midnight"
  "Mozart for Morning Coffee"
  "Mozart for Morning Meditation"
  "Mozart for Your Mind"
  "Mozart on the Menu"

Phillips Classics
Polygram Classics & Jazz
825 Eighth Avenue, 26th Floor
New York, NY, 10019, USA

Classical Music Resources ♪ ♪ ♪ ♪ ♪ ♪ ♪ ♪ ♪ ♪ ♪ ♪ ♪ ♪

Relax with the Classics

The LIND series focuses on early Baroque, with each CD offering a wide variety of music.

LIND Institute
PO Box 14487
San Francisco, CA, 94114, USA
<www.lind-institute.com>

The Mozart Effect—Music for Children

This series has varying moods and tempos, more like a sampler of the Baroque music than a collection for trainers.

The Children's Group
1400 Bayly Street, #7
Pickering, Ontario, Canada, L1W 3R2
<www.childrensgroup.com>

Don Gibson's Solitudes, Exploring Nature with Music

Natural sounds are featured on these CDs. In some cases, the nature sounds may distract from learning, but the CDs are well produced and are useful in appropriate situations.

Solitudes Ltd
1131A Leslie Street, Suite 500
Toronto, M3C 3L8, Canada

Classical Music Resources ♪ ♪ ♪ ♪ ♪ ♪ ♪ ♪ ♪ ♪(continued)

Nimbus Records

Nimus is a supplier of CDs in the U.K. Their catalog is not specifically designed for trainers, but they do offer a wide selection of classical music.

Nimus Records
Wyastone Leys, Monmouth, NP5 35R, U.K.
<www.nimbus.ltd.uk>

The Alpha Relaxation System

This series focuses on brain wave research and its application to music CDs. The material can encourage specific brain wave patterns, but it does not feature recognizable musical material.

The Relaxation Company
PO Box 305
Roslyn, NY, 11576, USA
(800) 788-6670

5. Other Music Resources

New Age Music

The Forte Series. Michael C's forte series is a collection of original music that soars. The music is smart, lyrical, and well constructed.

Titles:
"Colors"
"Above the Clouds"
"Sunburst"
"Romantic Piano"
"Classics for the Soul"
"Ivory Blue"

World Music Group Inc.
3319 West End Avenue, Suite 200
Nashville, TN, 71324, USA
(888) 647-6655

Windham Hill Records. Windham Hill specializes in New Age compilations that are perfect for any trainer building a library of CDs on a budget. Compilations, by their very nature, offer trainers all the best music an artist has to offer in one CD.

Titles:
"All the Seasons of George Winston"
"The Best of Yanni, Devotion"
"Paint the Sky with Stars: The Best of Enya"

Windham Hill Records
PO Box 5501
Beverly Hills, CA 90209
United States of America

5. Other Music Resources ♪ ♪ ♪ ♪ ♪ ♪ ♪ ♪ ♪ ♪(continued)

BMG Record Music Services. Perhaps the easiest way for a trainer to compile the music required for training with a beat is to join a music service. BMG is one of many such services available, including Columbia House, and Britannia.

> BMG
> PO Box 1958
> Indianapolis, IN 46291
> United States of America
> <www.bmgmusicservice.com>

Other resources might include your neighborhood record store, on-line music-recording sales companies, and your local library.

Royalty-Free Music Sources

Royalty-free music companies write, arrange, and record generic instrumental music. Because the music is entirely written and produced by the selling company, the purchaser can, within limits, use the music in most contexts without additional royalty fees.

The Music Bakery. The Music Bakery specializes in high-quality thematic music. Musical styles include classical, high tech, New Age, jazz, rock, country, historical/geographical, ethnic, sports, and industrial. Selections are provided in thirty- and sixty-second and longer segments.

> The Music Bakery
> 7522 Campbell Rd., #113-2
> Dallas, Texas, 75248, USA
> (800) 229-0313
> (615) 790-9897
> <www.musicbakery.com>

5. Other Music Resources ♪ ♪ ♪ ♪ ♪ ♪ ♪ ♪ ♪ ♪ ♪ ♪ ♪ ♪ ♪

Network Music LLC. Network Music focuses on a contemporary sound, while maintaining a large library of past styles. Their library can meet virtually any need in a wide variety of musical styles. An added bonus is Network Music's presence in several different countries.

USA:

Network Music LLC
15150 Avenue of Science
San Diego, CA 92128
(858) 451-6400
(800) 854-2075
<www.networkmusic.com>

Europe:

Network Music Europe
Wilhelminapark 1
2012 KA Haarlem
Netherlands
31-23-5-312-655

Australia:

EMI Music Publishing
1 Gurrigal Street
Mosman, NSW 2088
61-2-9960-5400

5. Other Music Resources ♪ ♪ ♪ ♪ ♪ ♪ ♪ ♪ ♪ ♪(continued)

Music Rights Organizations

A music-performing rights organization represents songwriters; film, television, musical theater, and classical music composers; and music publishers. Typically, performing rights organizations collect royalties from businesses that use that music in the course of their daily activities. The organization then distributes that money to the composers and publishers of the musical works. Music-performing rights organizations exist in virtually every country. Some of the primary organizations are listed below.

Australia

The Australasian Performing Right Association Limited (APRA)
Locked Bag 3456
St Leonards, NSW 2065
61-2-9935-7700
<www.apra.com.au>

Canada

Canadian Musical Reproduction Rights Agency Ltd. (CMRRA)
56 Wellesley Street W. #320
Toronto, Ontario M5S 2S3
(416) 926-1966
<www.cmrra.ca>

Society of Authors, Composers, and Music Publishers of Canada (SOCAN)
41 Valleybrook Drive
Don Mills, Ontario M3B 2S6
(416) 445-8700

5. Other Music Resources ♪ ♪ ♪ ♪ ♪ ♪ ♪ ♪ ♪ ♪ ♪ ♪ ♪ ♪

Ireland

Irish Music Rights Organisation Copyright House (IMRO)
Pembroke Row
Lower Baggot Street
Dublin 2
353 (0) 1-661-4844
<www.imro.ie>

United Kingdom

Authors' Licensing & Collecting Society (ALCS)
Marlborough Court, 14-18 Holborn, London EC1N 2LE
Telephone: 44 (0) 171-395-0600
<www.alcs.co.uk>

Mechanical Copyright Protection Society (MCPS)
Elgar House
41 Streatham High Road
London SW16 1ER
020-8664-4400
<www.mcps.co.uk>

Performing Right Society Copyright House (PRS)
29/33 Berners Street
London W1P 4AA
020-7580-5544
<www.prs.co.uk>

United States

The American Society of Composers, Authors, and Publishers
(ASCAP)
One Lincoln Plaza
New York, NY 10023
(212) 621-6000

5. Other Music Resources ♪ ♪ ♪ ♪ ♪ ♪ ♪ ♪ ♪ ♪(continued)

ASCAP Satellite Office

8 Cork Street
London W1X 1PB
011-44-171-439-0909

Broadcast Music Inc. (BMI)
320 West 57th Street
New York, NY 10019-3790
(212) 586-2000
<www.bmi.com>

BMI Satellite Office

84 Harley House
Marylebone Road
London NW1 5HN, England
011-44171-486-2036

Umbrella Organizations

BIEM
14 Rue Lincoln
75008 Paris
France
33-1-5393-6700
<ourworld.compuserve.com/homepages/biem>
Representatives in thirty countries

The International Confederation of Societies of Authors and
Composers (CISAC)
11 rue Kepler
75116 Paris
France
33-1-53-57-34-00
<www.cisac.org>
Representatives in eighty-seven countries

6. Pop Placement by Song

"ABC"	The Jackson 5
"Abracadabra"	The Steve Miller Band
"Ain't No Mountain High Enough"	Marvin Gaye and Tammi Terrell
"All Right Now"	Free
"All Things Must Pass"	George Harrison
"All You Need Is Love"	The Beatles
"Aquarius/Let the Sunshine In"	The 5th Dimension
"Back Stabbers"	The O'Jays
"Bad, Bad Leroy Brown"	Jim Croce
"Bad Moon Rising"	Credence Clearwater Revival
"Banana Boat"	Harry Belafonte
"Beat Goes On"	Sonny and Cher
"Beat It"	Michael Jackson
"Big Shot"	Billy Joel
"Black & White"	Three Dog Night
"Born to Be Alive"	Patrick Hernandez
"Both Sides Now"	Judy Collins
"Burning Down the House"	The Talking Heads
"Call Me"	Blondie
"Can't Buy Me Love"	The Beatles
"Car Wash"	Rose Royce
"Catch Us if You Can"	The Dave Clark Five
"Celebrate"	Three Dog Night
"Celebration"	Kool and the Gang
"Chain Gang"	Sam Cooke
"Changes"	David Bowie
"Circle of Life"	Elton John
"Come and Get It"	Badfinger
"Coming Up"	Paul McCartney
"Crossroads"	Cream
"Dancing in the Street"	Martha and the Vandellas
"Ding Dong the Witch Is Dead"	The Fifth Estate
"Disco Inferno"	The Trammps

6. Pop Placement by Song ♪ ♪ ♪ ♪ ♪ ♪ ♪ ♪ ♪ ♪(continued)

"Doctor My Eyes"	Jackson Browne
"Don't Ask Me Why"	Billy Joel
"Don't Let Me Be Misunderstood"	The Animals
"Don't Stop"	Fleetwood Mac
"Don't Worry Be Happy"	Bobby McFerrin
"Draggin' the Line"	Tommy James
"Eleanor Rigby"	The Beatles
"Everybody Have Fun Tonight"	Wang Chung
"Everybody Is a Star"	Sly and the Family Stone
"Everybody Wants to Rule the World"	Tears for Fears
"Everyday People"	Sly and the Family Stone
"Everything Is Beautiful"	Ray Stevens
"Express Yourself"	Madonna
"Eye of the Tiger"	Survivor
"Fame"	David Bowie
"Fame"	Irene Cara
"Feel Like a Number"	Bob Seger and the Silver Bullet Band
"Fly Like an Eagle"	Steve Miller
"Footloose"	Kenny Loggins
"Freedom"	Wham! George Michael
"Funkytown"	Lipps, Inc. Pseudo Echo
"Get a Job"	The Silhouettes
"Get Back"	The Beatles
"Get Down on It"	Kool and the Gang
"Get Together"	The Youngbloods
"Ghostbusters"	Ray Parker Jr.
"Girls Just Want to Have Fun"	Cyndi Lauper
"Give Me Just a Little More Time"	The Chairmen of the Board
"Gonna' Fly Now"	Bill Conti Maynard Ferguson
"Good Times"	Chic
"Good Vibrations"	The Beach Boys
"The Greatest Love of All"	Whitney Houston
"A Hard Day's Night"	The Beatles

6. Pop Placement by Song ♪ ♪ ♪ ♪ ♪ ♪ ♪ ♪ ♪ ♪ ♪ ♪ ♪ ♪ ♪ ♪

"Heart of Rock and Roll"	Huey Lewis and the News
"The Heat Is On"	Glenn Frey
"Help!"	The Beatles
"Help Me Rhonda"	The Beach Boys
"Hey Jude"	The Beatles
"Hit Me with Your Best Shot"	Pat Benatar
"Hit the Road Jack"	Ray Charles
"Hold On! I'm Coming"	Sam and Dave
"Hold Your Head Up"	Argent
"Holiday"	Madonna
"The Hustle"	Van McCoy
"I Can Help"	Billy Swan
"I Can See Clearly Now"	Johnny Nash
"(I Can't Get No) Satisfaction"	The Rolling Stones
"I Can't Go for That (No Can Do)"	Hall and Oates
"I Feel Free"	Cream
"I Get Around"	The Beach Boys
"I Got You (I Feel Good)"	James Brown
"I Heard It through the Grapevine"	Marvin Gaye
"I Just Want to Celebrate"	Rare Earth
"I'll Be There"	The Jackson 5
"I'll Tumble 4 Ya"	Culture Club
"I'm a Believer"	The Monkees
"I'm Alright"	Kenny Loggins
"I'm So Excited"	The Pointer Sisters
"It Don't Come Easy"	Ringo Starr
"I Thank You"	Sam and Dave
"It's Still Rock and Roll to Me"	Billy Joel
"It's Your Thing"	The Isley Brothers
"I Will Survive"	Gloria Gaynor
"I Wish"	Stevie Wonder
"Jailhouse Rock"	Elvis Presley
"Jive Talkin'"	The Bee Gees
"Joy to the World"	Three Dog Night
"(Just Like) Starting Over"	John Lennon
"Ladies Night"	Kool and the Gang

6. Pop Placement by Song ♪ ♪ ♪ ♪ ♪ ♪ ♪ ♪ ♪ ♪(continued)

"Lean on Me"	Bill Withers
	Club Nouveau
"Le Freak"	Chic
"Let It Be"	The Beatles
"Let's Go Crazy"	Prince
"The Lion Sleeps Tonight"	The Tokens
"The Logical Song"	Supertramp
"Man in the Mirror"	Michael Jackson
"Material Girl"	Madonna
"A Matter of Trust"	Billy Joel
"Monday, Monday"	The Mamas and the Papas
"Money (That's What I Want)"	Barrett Strong
"Morning Train (9 to 5)"	Sheena Easton
"My Life"	Billy Joel
"My Prerogative"	Bobby Brown
"Nightshift"	The Commodores
"**1999**"	Prince
"9 to 5"	Dolly Parton
"Nothing from Nothing"	Billy Preston
"No Time"	Guess Who
"Old Time Rock and Roll"	Bob Seger
"Our Day Will Come"	Ruby and the Romantics
	Frankie Valli
"People Got to Be Free"	The Rascals
"Pick Up the Pieces"	Average White Band
"Play That Funky Music"	Wild Cherry
"The Power of Love"	Huey Lewis and the News
"Pressure"	Billy Joel
"Put a Little Love in Your Heart"	Jackie DeShannon
	Annie Lennox and Al Greene
"Reach Out I'll Be There"	The Four Tops
	Diana Ross
"Respect"	Aretha Franklin
"Rock On"	David Essex
"The Safety Dance"	Men without Hats
"Seasons in the Sun"	Terry Jacks
"See You Later, Alligator"	Bill Haley and His Comets

6. Pop Placement by Song

"She Blinded Me with Science"   Thomas Dolby
"Shining Star"   Earth, Wind and Fire
"Short People"   Randy Newman

"Sixteen Tons"   "Tennessee" Ernie Ford
"Something to Talk About"   Bonnie Raitt
"Stand by Me"   Ben E. King

"Stay"   Maurice Williams and the Zodiacs
"Stayin' Alive"   The Bee Gees
"Take Five"   Dave Brubeck Quartet

"Takin' Care of Business"   Bachman-Turner Overdrive
"Thank You (Falettinme Be Mice
    Elf Agin)"   Sly and the Family Stone
"That'll Be the Day"   Buddy Holly/The Crickets

"That's What Friends Are For"   Dionne and Friends
"Things That Make You
    Go Hmmmm . . ."   C & C Music Factory
"The Tide Is High"   Blondie

"Tighten Up"   Archie Bell and the Drells
"Time after Time"   Cyndi Lauper
"Time in a Bottle"   Jim Croce

"The Time of My Life"   Bill Medley and Jennifer Warnes
"Tired of Toein' the Line"   Rocky Brunette
"Tossin' and Turnin'"   Bobby Lewis

"True Colors"   Cyndi Lauper
"Turn, Turn, Turn"   The Byrds
"Unbelievable"   EMF

"Upside Down"   Diana Ross
"We Are Family"   Sister Sledge
"We Are the Champions"   Queen

"We Are the World"   USA for Africa
"We Can Work It Out"   The Beatles
"We Didn't Start the Fire"   Billy Joel

"We'll Sing in the Sunshine"   Gale Garnett
"(We're Gonna) Rock around
    the Clock"   Bill Haley and His Comets
"We're Not Gonna Take It"   Twisted Sister

6. Pop Placement by Song ♪ ♪ ♪ ♪ ♪ ♪ ♪ ♪ ♪ ♪ (continued)

"Whatever Will Be, Will Be (Que Sera, Sera)"	Doris Day
"Whip It"	Devo
"Will It Go Round in Circles"	Billy Preston
"Wind beneath My Wings"	Bette Midler
"With a Little Help from My Friends"	The Beatles
"With a Little Luck"	Wings
"Wonderful World"	Sam Cooke
"Working for the Weekend"	Loverboy
"Working in the Coal Mine"	Devo
	Lee Dorsey
"Working My Way back to You"	The 4 Seasons
"You Are the Sunshine of My Life"	Stevie Wonder
"You Can't Always Get What You Want"	The Rolling Stones
"You Needed Me"	Anne Murray
"You've Got a Friend"	Carole King
	James Taylor

SOURCE: Whitburn, J. (1996). *The Billboard Book of Top Hits,* 6th ed. New York: Billboard Publications.

7. Pop Placement by Artist

The Animals	"Don't Let Me Be Misunderstood"
Argent	"Hold Your Head Up"
Average White Band	"Pick Up the Pieces"
Bachman-Turner Overdrive	"Takin' Care of Business"
Badfinger	"Come and Get It"
The Beach Boys	"Good Vibrations"
	"Help Me Rhonda"
	"I Get Around"
The Beatles	"All You Need Is Love"
	"Can't Buy Me Love"
	"Eleanor Rigby"
	"Get Back"
	"A Hard Day's Night"
	"Help!"
	"Hey Jude"
	"Let It Be"
	"We Can Work It Out"
	"With a Little Help from My Friends"
The Bee Gees	"Jive Talkin'"
	"Stayin' Alive"
Harry Belafonte	"Banana Boat"
Archie Bell and the Drells	"Tighten Up"
Pat Benatar	"Hit Me with Your Best Shot"
Blondie	"Call Me"
	"The Tide Is High"
David Bowie	"Changes"
	"Fame"
Bobby Brown	"My Prerogative"
James Brown	"I Got You (I Feel Good)"
Jackson Browne	"Doctor My Eyes"
Rocky Brunette	"Tired of Toein' the Line"
The Byrds	"Turn, Turn, Turn"
C & C Music Factory	"Things That Make You Go Hmmmm . . ."
Irene Cara	"Fame"
The Chairmen of the Board	"Give Me Just a Little More Time"
Ray Charles	"Hit the Road Jack"

7. Pop Placement by Artist ♪ ♪ ♪ ♪ ♪ ♪ ♪ ♪ ♪ ♪(continued)

Chic	"Good Times"
	"Le Freak"
Bill Conti	"Gonna' Fly Now"
Sam Cooke	"Chain Gang"
	"Wonderful World"
Club Nouveau	"Lean on Me"
Judy Collins	"Both Sides Now"
The Commodores	"Nightshift"
Cream	"Crossroads"
	"I Feel Free"
Credence Clearwater Revival	"Bad Moon Rising"
Jim Croce	"Bad, Bad Leroy Brown"
	"Time in a Bottle"
Culture Club	"I'll Tumble 4 Ya"
Dave Brubeck Quartet	"Take Five"
The Dave Clark Five	"Catch Us if You Can"
Doris Day	"Whatever Will Be, Will Be (Que Sera, Sera)"
Jackie DeShannon	"Put a Little Love in Your Heart"
Devo	"Whip It"
	"Working in the Coal Mine"
Dionne and Friends	"That's What Friends Are For"
Thomas Dolby	"She Blinded Me with Science"
Lee Dorsey	"Working in the Coal Mine"
Earth, Wind and Fire	"Shining Star"
Sheena Easton	"Morning Train (9 to 5)"
EMF	"Unbelievable"
David Essex	"Rock On"
Maynard Ferguson	"Gonna' Fly Now"
The 5th Dimension	"Aquarius/Let the Sunshine In"
The Fifth Estate	"Ding Dong the Witch Is Dead"
Fleetwood Mac	"Don't Stop"
"Tennessee" Ernie Ford	"Sixteen Tons"
The 4 Seasons	"Working My Way Back to You"
The Four Tops	"Reach Out I'll Be There"
Aretha Franklin	"Respect"
Free	"All Right Now"
Glenn Frey	"The Heat Is On"
Gale Garnett	"We'll Sing in the Sunshine"
Marvin Gaye	"I Heard It through the Grapevine"

7. Pop Placement by Artist ♪ ♪ ♪ ♪ ♪ ♪ ♪ ♪ ♪ ♪ ♪ ♪ ♪ ♪

Marvin Gaye and Tammi Terrell	"Ain't No Mountain High Enough"
Gloria Gaynor	"I Will Survive"
Al Greene and Annie Lennox	"Put a Little Love in Your Heart"
Guess Who	"No Time"
Bill Haley and His Comets	"(We're Gonna) Rock around the Clock"
	"See You Later, Alligator"
Hall and Oates	"I Can't Go for That (No Can Do)"
George Harrison	"All Things Must Pass"
Patrick Hernandez	"Born to Be Alive"
Buddy Holly/The Crickets	"That'll Be the Day"
Whitney Houston	"The Greatest Love of All"
The Isley Brothers	"It's Your Thing"
Terry Jacks	"Seasons in the Sun"
Michael Jackson	"Beat It"
	"Man in the Mirror"
The Jackson 5	"ABC"
	"I'll Be There"
Tommy James	"Draggin' the Line"
Billy Joel	"A Matter of Trust"
	"Big Shot"
	"Don't Ask Me Why"
	"It's Still Rock and Roll to Me"
	"My Life"
	"Pressure"
	"We Didn't Start the Fire"
Elton John	"Circle of Life"
Ben E. King	"Stand by Me"
Carole King	"You've Got a Friend"
Kool and the Gang	"Celebration"
	"Ladies Night"
	"Get Down on It"
Cyndi Lauper	"Girls Just Want to Have Fun"
	"Time after Time"
	"True Colors"
John Lennon	"(Just Like) Starting Over"
Annie Lennox and Al Greene	"Put a Little Love in Your Heart"
Bobby Lewis	"Tossin' and Turnin'"
Huey Lewis and the News	"Heart of Rock and Roll"
	"The Power of Love"

7. Pop Placement by Artist ♪ ♪ ♪ ♪ ♪ ♪ ♪ ♪ ♪ ♪ (continued)

Lipps, Inc.	"Funkytown"
Kenny Loggins	"I'm Alright"
	"Footloose"
Loverboy	"Working for the Weekend"
Madonna	"Express Yourself"
	"Holiday"
	"Material Girl"
The Mamas and the Papas	"Monday, Monday"
Martha and the Vandellas	"Dancing in the Street"
Paul McCartney	"Coming Up"
Van McCoy	"The Hustle"
Bobby McFerrin	"Don't Worry Be Happy"
Bill Medley and Jennifer Warnes	"The Time of My Life"
Men without Hats	"The Safety Dance"
George Michael	"Freedom"
Bette Midler	"Wind beneath My Wings"
Steve Miller	"Fly Like an Eagle"
	"Abracadabra"
The Monkees	"I'm a Believer"
Anne Murray	"You Needed Me"
Johnny Nash	"I Can See Clearly Now"
Randy Newman	"Short People"
The O'Jays	"Back Stabbers"
Ray Parker Jr.	"Ghostbusters"
Dolly Parton	"9 to 5"
The Pointer Sisters	"I'm So Excited"
Elvis Presley	"Jailhouse Rock"
Billy Preston	"Nothing from Nothing"
	"Will It Go Round in Circles"
Prince	"Let's Go Crazy"
	"**1999**"
Pseudo Echo	"Funkytown"
Queen	"We Are the Champions"
Bonnie Raitt	"Something to Talk About"
Rare Earth	"I Just Want to Celebrate"
The Rascals	"People Got to Be Free"
The Rolling Stones	"Emotional Rescue"
	"(I Can't Get No) Satisfaction"
	"You Can't Always Get What You Want"

7. Pop Placement by Artist ♪ ♪ ♪ ♪ ♪ ♪ ♪ ♪ ♪ ♪ ♪ ♪ ♪ ♪

Diana Ross	"Reach Out I'll Be There"
	"Upside Down"
Rose Royce	"Car Wash"
Ruby and the Romantics	"Our Day Will Come"
Sam and Dave	"Hold On! I'm Coming"
	"I Thank You"
Bob Seger	"Feel Like a Number"
	"Old Time Rock and Roll"
The Silhouettes	"Get a Job"
Sister Sledge	"We Are Family"
Sly and the Family Stone	"Everybody Is a Star"
	"Everyday People"
	"Thank You (Falettinme Be Mice Elf Agin)"
Sonny and Cher	"Beat Goes On"
Ringo Starr	"It Don't Come Easy"
Ray Stevens	"Everything Is Beautiful"
Barrett Strong	"Money (That's What I Want)"
Supertramp	"The Logical Song"
Survivor	"Eye of the Tiger"
Billy Swan	"I Can Help"
The Talking Heads	"Burning Down the House"
Tammi Terrell and Marvin Gaye	"Ain't No Mountain High Enough"
James Taylor	"You've Got a Friend"
Tears for Fears	"Everybody Wants to Rule the World"
Three Dog Night	"Black & White"
	"Celebrate"
	"Joy to the World"
The Tokens	"The Lion Sleeps Tonight"
The Trammps	"Disco Inferno"
Twisted Sister	"We're Not Gonna Take It"
USA for Africa	"We Are the World"
Frankie Valli	"Our Day Will Come"
Wang Chung	"Everybody Have Fun Tonight"
Jennifer Warnes and Bill Medley	"The Time of My Life"
Wham!	"Freedom"
Wild Cherry	"Play That Funky Music"
Maurice Williams and the Zodiacs	"Stay"
Wings	"With a Little Luck"

7. Pop Placement by Artist ♪ ♪ ♪ ♪ ♪ ♪ ♪ ♪ ♪ (continued)

Bill Withers . . . . "Lean on Me"
Stevie Wonder . . . . "I Wish"
                               "You Are the Sunshine of My Life"
The Youngbloods . . . . "Get Together"

SOURCE: Whitburn, J. (1996). *The Billboard Book of Top Hits,* 6th ed. New York: Billboard Publications.

8. Pop Placement by Function

Any listing of this sort is, by its nature, subjective. Various songs will serve different purposes, according to the needs of your training environment. Use the listings below as a possible starting point for your instruction, and, using your best judgment, match specific songs to your learning situation.

Breaks

"Pick Up the Pieces"	Average White Band
"See You Later, Alligator"	Bill Haley and His Comets
"Stay"	Maurice Williams and the Zodiacs
"Take Five"	Dave Brubeck Quartet

Career Management

"All Things Must Pass"	George Harrison
"Aquarius/Let the Sunshine In"	The 5th Dimension
"Born to Be Alive"	Patrick Hernandez
"Both Sides Now"	Judy Collins
"Circle of Life"	Elton John
"Come and Get It"	Badfinger
"Coming Up"	Paul McCartney
"Don't Stop"	Fleetwood Mac
"Don't Worry Be Happy"	Bobby McFerrin
"Emotional Rescue"	The Rolling Stones
"Everybody Wants to Rule the World"	Tears for Fears
"Fame"	David Bowie
"Fame"	Irene Cara
"Fly Like an Eagle"	Steve Miller
"Freedom"	Wham!
	George Michael
"Funkytown"	Lipps, Inc.
	Pseudo Echo
"Get Back"	The Beatles
"Get Down on It"	Kool and the Gang
"Gonna' Fly Now"	Bill Conti
	Maynard Ferguson

8. Pop Placement by Function ♪ ♪ ♪ ♪ ♪ ♪ ♪ ♪ ♪(continued)

Career Management *(continued)*

"Help!"	The Beatles
"Hit the Road Jack"	Ray Charles
"Hold Your Head Up"	Argent
"I Can See Clearly Now"	Johnny Nash
"(I Can't Get No) Satisfaction"	The Rolling Stones
"I Can't Go for That (No Can Do)"	Hall and Oates
"I Feel Free"	Cream
"I Get Around"	The Beach Boys
"I'm Alright"	Kenny Loggins
"It Don't Come Easy"	Ringo Starr
"It's Your Thing"	The Isley Brothers
"I Will Survive"	Gloria Gaynor
"I Wish"	Stevie Wonder
"(Just Like) Starting Over"	John Lennon
"Man in the Mirror"	Michael Jackson
"Monday, Monday"	The Mamas and the Papas
"Money (That's What I Want)"	Barrett Strong
"My Life"	Billy Joel
"My Prerogative"	Bobby Brown
"Our Day Will Come"	Ruby and the Romantics Frankie Valli
"Pick Up the Pieces"	Average White Band
"Play That Funky Music"	Wild Cherry
"Pressure"	Billy Joel
"Rock On"	David Essex
"Shining Star"	Earth, Wind and Fire
"Stayin' Alive"	The Bee Gees
"Takin' Care of Business"	Bachman-Turner Overdrive
"Things That Make You Go Hmmmm..."	C & C Music Factory
"Tighten Up"	Archie Bell and the Drells
"Tired of Toein' the Line"	Rocky Brunette
"Tossin' and Turnin'"	Bobby Lewis
"Turn, Turn, Turn"	The Byrds
"Upside Down"	Diana Ross

8. Pop Placement by Function

"We Didn't Start the Fire"	Billy Joel
"We're Not Gonna Take It"	Twisted Sister
"Whatever Will Be, Will Be (Que Sera, Sera)"	Doris Day
"Whip It"	Devo
"Will It Go Round in Circles"	Billy Preston
"You Can't Always Get What You Want"	The Rolling Stones

Celebrations

"Celebrate"	Three Dog Night
"Celebration"	Kool and the Gang
"Circle of Life"	Elton John
"Dancing in the Street"	Martha and the Vandellas
"Ding Dong the Witch Is Dead"	The Fifth Estate
"Don't Stop"	Fleetwood Mac
"Don't Worry Be Happy"	Bobby McFerrin
"Everybody Have Fun Tonight"	Wang Chung
"Fly Like an Eagle"	Steve Miller
"Footloose"	Kenny Loggins
"Get Down on It"	Kool and the Gang
"Girls Just Want to Have Fun"	Cyndi Lauper
"Gonna' Fly Now"	Bill Conti
	Maynard Ferguson
"Good Times"	Chic
"Good Vibrations"	The Beach Boys
"Holiday"	Madonna
"I Feel Free"	Cream
"I Got You (I Feel Good)"	James Brown
"I Just Want to Celebrate"	Rare Earth
"I'm So Excited"	The Pointer Sisters
"I Thank You"	Sam and Dave
"Joy to the World"	Three Dog Night
"Ladies Night"	Kool and the Gang
"Let's Go Crazy"	Prince

8. Pop Placement by Function ♪ ♪ ♪ ♪ ♪ ♪ ♪ ♪ ♪(continued)

Celebrations (continued)

"**1999**"	Prince
"Old Time Rock and Roll"	Bob Seger
"Seasons in the Sun"	Terry Jacks
"The Time of My Life"	Jennifer Warnes and Bill Medley
"We Are Family"	Sister Sledge
"We Are the Champions"	Queen

Communication

"Back Stabbers"	The O'Jays
"Beat It"	Michael Jackson
"Call Me"	Blondie
"Don't Let Me Be Misunderstood"	The Animals
"Express Yourself"	Madonna
"I Can't Go for That (No Can Do)"	Hall and Oates
"I Heard It through the Grapevine"	Marvin Gaye
"Jive Talkin'"	The Bee Gees
"A Matter of Trust"	Billy Joel
"People Got to Be Free"	The Rascals
"She Blinded Me with Science"	Thomas Dolby
"Something to Talk About"	Bonnie Raitt
"Stand by Me"	Ben E. King
"We Can Work It Out"	The Beatles

Computer/Technical Training

"ABC"	The Jackson 5
"Changes"	David Bowie
"Feel Like a Number"	Bob Seger and the Silver Bullet Band
"Get Down on It"	Kool and the Gang
"Give Me Just a Little More Time"	The Chairmen of the Board
"I Get Around"	The Beach Boys
"(Just Like) Starting Over"	John Lennon
"The Logical Song"	Supertramp

8. Pop Placement by Function ♪ ♪ ♪ ♪ ♪ ♪ ♪ ♪ ♪ ♪ ♪ ♪

Customer Service

"ABC"	The Jackson 5
"Ain't No Mountain High Enough"	Marvin Gaye and Tammi Terrell
"All Right Now"	Free
"Call Me"	Blondie
"Come and Get It"	Badfinger
"Doctor My Eyes"	Jackson Browne
"Don't Let Me Be Misunderstood"	The Animals
"Don't Worry Be Happy"	Bobby McFerrin
"Everybody Have Fun Tonight"	Wang Chung
"Everybody Is a Star"	Sly and the Family Stone
"Everyday People"	Sly and the Family Stone
"Everything Is Beautiful"	Ray Stevens
"Express Yourself"	Madonna
"Feel Like a Number"	Bob Seger and the Silver Bullet Band
"Get Together"	The Youngbloods
"Ghostbusters"	Ray Parker Jr.
"Give Me Just a Little More Time"	The Chairmen of the Board
"Good Times"	Chic
"Good Vibrations"	The Beach Boys
"Help!"	The Beatles
"Help Me Rhonda"	The Beach Boys
"Hey Jude"	The Beatles
"Hold On! I'm Coming"	Sam and Dave
"I Can Help"	Billy Swan
"I Can See Clearly Now"	Johnny Nash
"I'll Be There"	The Jackson 5
"I'll Tumble 4 Ya"	Culture Club
"It's Your Thing"	The Isley Brothers
"Lean on Me"	Bill Withers
	Club Nouveau
"Let It Be"	The Beatles
"A Matter of Trust"	Billy Joel
"Pick Up the Pieces"	Average White Band
"The Power of Love"	Huey Lewis and the News

8. Pop Placement by Function ♪ ♪ ♪ ♪ ♪ ♪ ♪ ♪ ♪(continued)

Customer Service (continued)

"Put a Little Love in Your Heart"	Jackie DeShannon Annie Lennox and Al Greene
"Reach Out I'll Be There"	The Four Tops Diana Ross
"Respect"	Aretha Franklin
"Shining Star"	Earth, Wind and Fire
"Stand by Me"	Ben E. King
"That's What Friends Are For"	Dionne and Friends
"Things That Make You Go Hmmmm . . ."	C & C Music Factory
"The Time of My Life"	Jennifer Warnes and Bill Medley
"True Colors"	Cyndi Lauper
"We Can Work It Out"	The Beatles
"With a Little Help from My Friends"	The Beatles
"You've Got a Friend"	Carole King James Taylor

Diversity/Sexual Harassment

"Black & White"	Three Dog Night
"Born to Be Alive"	Patrick Hernandez
"Both Sides Now"	Judy Collins
"Circle of Life"	Elton John
"Everybody Is a Star"	Sly and the Family Stone
"Everyday People"	Sly and the Family Stone
"Everything Is Beautiful"	Ray Stevens
"The Greatest Love of All"	Whitney Houston
"It's Your Thing"	The Isley Brothers
"I Will Survive"	Gloria Gaynor
"Ladies Night"	Kool and the Gang
"Man in the Mirror"	Michael Jackson
"A Matter of Trust"	Billy Joel
"People Got to Be Free"	The Rascals
"The Power of Love"	Huey Lewis and the News

8. Pop Placement by Function ♪ ♪ ♪ ♪ ♪ ♪ ♪ ♪ ♪ ♪ ♪ ♪

"Put a Little Love in Your Heart"	Jackie DeShannon Annie Lennox and Al Greene
"Respect"	Aretha Franklin
"Short People"	Randy Newman
"Thank You (Falettinme Be Mice Elf Agin)"	Sly and the Family Stone
"That's What Friends Are For"	Dionne and Friends
"Things That Make You Go Hmmmm . . ."	C & C Music Factory
"True Colors"	Cyndi Lauper
"Unbelievable"	EMF
"We Are Family"	Sister Sledge
"We Are the World"	USA for Africa
"We Can Work It Out"	The Beatles
"We're Not Gonna Take It"	Twisted Sister

Financial Training

"Can't Buy Me Love"	The Beatles
"Material Girl"	Madonna
"Money (That's What I Want)"	Barrett Strong
"Nothing from Nothing"	Billy Preston
"Takin' Care of Business"	Bachman-Turner Overdrive

Leadership

"Bad, Bad Leroy Brown"	Jim Croce
"Big Shot"	Billy Joel
"Both Sides Now"	Judy Collins
"Dancing in the Street"	Martha and the Vandellas
"Ding Dong the Witch Is Dead"	The Fifth Estate
"Don't Stop"	Fleetwood Mac
"Everybody Wants to Rule the World"	Tears for Fears
"Gonna' Fly Now"	Bill Conti Maynard Ferguson
"Good Vibrations"	The Beach Boys
"The Greatest Love of All"	Whitney Houston
"The Heat Is On"	Glenn Frey
"Hit Me with Your Best Shot"	Pat Benatar

8. Pop Placement by Function ♪ ♪ ♪ ♪ ♪ ♪ ♪ ♪ ♪(continued)

Leadership *(continued)*

"Hold On! I'm Coming"	Sam and Dave
"I Can Help"	Billy Swan
"I'll Be There"	The Jackson 5
"I'll Tumble 4 Ya"	Culture Club
"Man in the Mirror"	Michael Jackson
"A Matter of Trust"	Billy Joel
"Nothing from Nothing"	Billy Preston
"Pick Up the Pieces"	Average White Band
"Put a Little Love in Your Heart"	Jackie DeShannon
	Annie Lennox and Al Greene
"Reach Out I'll Be There"	The Four Tops
	Diana Ross
"She Blinded Me with Science"	Thomas Dolby
"Takin' Care of Business"	Bachman-Turner Overdrive
"Tighten Up"	Archie Bell and the Drells
"True Colors"	Cyndi Lauper

Organizational Change

During Change

"All Things Must Pass"	George Harrison
"Bad Moon Rising"	Credence Clearwater Revival
"Burning Down the House"	The Talking Heads
"Changes"	David Bowie
"Crossroads"	Cream
"Disco Inferno"	The Trammps
"Don't Ask Me Why"	Billy Joel
"Don't Stop"	Fleetwood Mac
"Emotional Rescue"	The Rolling Stones
"Everybody Wants to Rule the World"	Tears for Fears
"Eye of the Tiger"	Survivor
"Get Back"	The Beatles
"The Heat Is On"	Glenn Frey
"Hit Me with Your Best Shot"	Pat Benatar
"Hit the Road Jack"	Ray Charles

8. Pop Placement by Function ♪ ♪ ♪ ♪ ♪ ♪ ♪ ♪ ♪ ♪ ♪ ♪ ♪ ♪

"(I Can't Get No) Satisfaction"	The Rolling Stones
"I Can't Go for That (No Can Do)"	Hall and Oates
"It's Still Rock and Roll to Me"	Billy Joel
"The Logical Song"	Supertramp
"Monday, Monday"	The Mamas and the Papas
"Takin' Care of Business"	Bachman-Turner Overdrive
"Tighten Up"	Archie Bell and the Drells
"Unbelievable"	EMF
"Upside Down"	Diana Ross
"We Didn't Start the Fire"	Billy Joel
"Whip It"	Devo
"Will It Go Round in Circles"	Billy Preston
"With a Little Luck"	Wings

Post Change

"All Right Now"	Free
"Aquarius/Let the Sunshine In"	The 5th Dimension
"Both Sides Now"	Judy Collins
"Circle of Life"	Elton John
"Come and Get It"	Badfinger
"Coming Up"	Paul McCartney
"Ding Dong the Witch Is Dead"	The Fifth Estate
"Doctor My Eyes"	Jackson Browne
"Don't Worry Be Happy"	Bobby McFerrin
"Gonna' Fly Now"	Bill Conti / Maynard Ferguson
"Good Times"	Chic
"Good Vibrations"	The Beach Boys
"A Hard Day's Night"	The Beatles
"Hey Jude"	The Beatles
"I Can See Clearly Now"	Johnny Nash
"I Feel Free"	Cream
"I'm a Believer"	The Monkees
"I'm Alright"	Kenny Loggins
"I'm So Excited"	The Pointer Sisters
"(Just Like) Starting Over"	John Lennon
"Let It Be"	The Beatles

8. Pop Placement by Function ♪ ♪ ♪ ♪ ♪ ♪ ♪ ♪ ♪(continued)

Organizational Change *(continued)*

Post Change *(continued)*

"Pick Up the Pieces"	Average White Band
"Rock On"	David Essex
"Seasons in the Sun"	Terry Jacks
"Stayin' Alive"	The Bee Gees
"The Tide Is High"	Blondie
"Turn, Turn, Turn"	The Byrds
"We Are Family"	Sister Sledge
"We Are the Champions"	Queen
"We'll Sing in the Sunshine"	Gale Garnett
"You Can't Always Get What You Want"	The Rolling Stones

Quality Control

"Coming Up"	Paul McCartney
"Fly Like an Eagle"	Steve Miller
"Get Down on It"	Kool and the Gang
"The Heat Is On"	Glenn Frey
"Hold Your Head Up"	Argent
"It Don't Come Easy"	Ringo Starr
"Pressure"	Billy Joel
"The Safety Dance"	Men without Hats
"Takin' Care of Business"	Bachman-Turner Overdrive
"The Tide Is High"	Blondie
"Tighten Up"	Archie Bell and the Drells

Self-Esteem

"Don't Stop"	Fleetwood Mac
"Don't Worry Be Happy"	Bobby McFerrin
"Eleanor Rigby"	The Beatles
"Everybody Is a Star"	Sly and the Family Stone
"Everyday People"	Sly and the Family Stone
"Express Yourself"	Madonna

8. Pop Placement by Function ♪ ♪ ♪ ♪ ♪ ♪ ♪ ♪ ♪ ♪ ♪ ♪

"Feel Like a Number"	Bob Seger and the Silver Bullet Band
"Fly Like an Eagle"	Steve Miller
"Freedom"	Wham!
	George Michael
"Get Down on It"	Kool and the Gang
"Gonna' Fly Now"	Bill Conti
	Maynard Ferguson
"Hey Jude"	The Beatles
"Hold Your Head Up"	Argent
"I Can See Clearly Now"	Johnny Nash
"I Can't Go for That (No Can Do)"	Hall and Oates
"I Feel Free"	Cream
"I Got You (I Feel Good)"	James Brown
"I'm Alright"	Kenny Loggins
"(Just Like) Starting Over"	John Lennon
"Man in the Mirror"	Michael Jackson
"My Life"	Billy Joel
"My Prerogative"	Bobby Brown
"Our Day Will Come"	Ruby and the Romantics
	Frankie Valli
"People Got to Be Free"	The Rascals
"Pick Up the Pieces"	Average White Band
"Put a Little Love in Your Heart"	Jackie DeShannon
	Annie Lennox and Al Greene
"Rock On"	David Essex
"Shining Star"	Earth, Wind and Fire
"Stayin' Alive"	The Bee Gees
"That'll Be the Day"	Buddy Holly/The Crickets
"True Colors"	Cyndi Lauper
"We Are the Champions"	Queen
"We're Not Gonna Take It"	Twisted Sister
"Whip It"	Devo

Stress Management

"Bad Moon Rising"	Credence Clearwater Revival
"Don't Worry Be Happy"	Bobby McFerrin
"Emotional Rescue"	The Rolling Stones

8. Pop Placement by Function ♪ ♪ ♪ ♪ ♪ ♪ ♪ ♪ ♪(continued)

Stress Management *(continued)*

"Good Vibrations"	The Beach Boys
"Help!"	The Beatles
"I'm Alright"	Kenny Loggins
"I Will Survive"	Gloria Gaynor
"Pressure"	Billy Joel
"Stayin' Alive"	The Bee Gees
"Tighten Up"	Archie Bell and the Drells
"Tossin' and Turnin'"	Bobby Lewis
"Turn, Turn, Turn"	The Byrds
"Unbelievable"	EMF
"Upside Down"	Diana Ross
"We Can Work It Out"	The Beatles
"Whatever Will Be, Will Be (Que Sera, Sera)"	Doris Day
"Whip It"	Devo
"You Can't Always Get What You Want"	The Rolling Stones

Teamwork

"Ain't No Mountain High Enough"	Marvin Gaye and Tammi Terrell
"All You Need Is Love"	The Beatles
"Back Stabbers"	The O'Jays
"Beat It"	Michael Jackson
"Big Shot"	Billy Joel
"Call Me"	Blondie
"Circle of Life"	Elton John
"Everybody Is a Star"	Sly and the Family Stone
"Everybody Wants to Rule the World"	Tears for Fears
"Get Down on It"	Kool and the Gang
"Get Together"	The Youngbloods
"Ghostbusters"	Ray Parker Jr.
"Help!"	The Beatles
"Help Me Rhonda"	The Beach Boys
"Hold On! I'm Coming"	Sam and Dave

8. Pop Placement by Function ♪ ♪ ♪ ♪ ♪ ♪ ♪ ♪ ♪ ♪ ♪ ♪ ♪

"I Can Help"	Billy Swan
"I Got You (I Feel Good)"	James Brown
"I'll Be There"	The Jackson 5
"I'll Tumble 4 Ya"	Culture Club
"Lean on Me"	Bill Withers
	Club Nouveau
"Let It Be"	The Beatles
"The Power of Love"	Huey Lewis and the News
"Reach Out I'll Be There"	The Four Tops
	Diana Ross
"Stand by Me"	Ben E. King
"That's What Friends Are For"	Dionne and Friends
"We Are Family"	Sister Sledge
"We Are the Champions"	Queen
"We Are the World"	USA for Africa
"Wind beneath My Wings"	Bette Midler
"With a Little Help from My Friends"	The Beatles
"You Are the Sunshine of My Life"	Stevie Wonder
"You Needed Me"	Anne Murray
"You've Got a Friend"	Carole King
	James Taylor

Telephone Communication Training

"Abracadabra"	The Steve Miller Band
"Call Me"	Blondie
"Come and Get It"	Badfinger
"Don't Worry Be Happy"	Bobby McFerrin
"Hold On! I'm Coming"	Sam and Dave
"I Can Help"	Billy Swan
"I'll Tumble 4 Ya"	Culture Club
"Jive Talkin'"	The Bee Gees
"Lean on Me"	Bill Withers
	Club Nouveau
"See You Later, Alligator"	Bill Haley and His Comets
"Something to Talk About"	Bonnie Raitt

8. Pop Placement by Function ♪ ♪ ♪ ♪ ♪ ♪ ♪ ♪ ♪(continued)

Time Management

"The Beat Goes On"	Sonny and Cher
"Catch Us if You Can"	The Dave Clark Five
"Give Me Just a Little More Time"	The Chairmen of the Board
"A Hard Day's Night"	The Beatles
"The Heat Is On"	Glenn Frey
"No Time"	Guess Who
"Pressure"	Billy Joel
"Stay"	Maurice Williams and the Zodiacs
"Takin' Care of Business"	Bachman-Turner Overdrive
"Tighten Up"	Archie Bell and the Drells
"Time after Time"	Cyndi Lauper
"Time in a Bottle"	Jim Croce
"Tired of Toein' the Line"	Rocky Brunette
"We Can Work It Out"	The Beatles
"(We're Gonna) Rock around the Clock"	Bill Haley and His Comets

Work Environment

"Banana Boat"	Harry Belafonte
"Car Wash"	Rose Royce
"Chain Gang"	Sam Cooke
"Don't Worry Be Happy"	Bobby McFerrin
"Draggin' the Line"	Tommy James
"Everybody Have Fun Tonight"	Wang Chung
"Fly Like an Eagle"	Steve Miller
"Get a Job"	The Silhouettes
"A Hard Day's Night"	The Beatles
"The Heat Is On"	Glenn Frey
"The Hustle"	Van McCoy
"Jailhouse Rock"	Elvis Presley
"Material Girl"	Madonna
"Morning Train (9 to 5)"	Sheena Easton
"Nightshift"	The Commodores
"9 to 5"	Dolly Parton
"Sixteen Tons"	"Tennessee" Ernie Ford
"Stayin' Alive"	The Bee Gees

8. Pop Placement by Function ♪ ♪ ♪ ♪ ♪ ♪ ♪ ♪ ♪ ♪ ♪ ♪ ♪

"Takin' Care of Business"	Bachman-Turner Overdrive
"Tired of Toein' the Line"	Rocky Brunette
"(We're Gonna) Rock around the Clock"	Bill Haley and His Comets
"With a Little Help from My Friends"	The Beatles
"Working for the Weekend"	Loverboy
"Working in the Coal Mine"	Devo
	Lee Dorsey
"Working My Way back to You"	The 4 Seasons
"You Can't Always Get What You Want"	The Rolling Stones

Training

"ABC"	The Jackson 5
"Abracadabra"	The Steve Miller Band
"Call Me"	Blondie
"Come and Get It"	Badfinger
"Get Down on It"	Kool and the Gang
"A Hard Day's Night"	The Beatles
"I Got You (I Feel Good)"	James Brown
"I'll Be There"	The Jackson 5
"I'll Tumble 4 Ya"	Culture Club
"Pressure"	Billy Joel
"The Safety Dance"	Men without Hats
"Stay"	Maurice Williams and the Zodiacs
"Tighten Up"	Archie Bell and the Drells
"Wonderful World"	Sam Cooke

SOURCE: Whitburn, J. (1996). *The Billboard Book of Top Hits,* 6th ed. New York: Billboard Publications.

9. Music Placement Matrix

	Baroque	Classical Period	Sound Tracks	Popular	New Age	Major Keys	Minor Keys	$\frac{4}{4}$	$\frac{3}{4}$	Fast	Slow
Start of Session	X	X	X	X	X	X		X	X	X	
Set a Theme	X	X	X	X	X	X	X	X	X	X	X
Creativity	X	X	X		X	X	X	X		X	X
Memorization	X	X				X	X	X			X
Relaxation	X	X			X		X	X	X		X
Background	X	X	X		X	X	X	X		X	X
Games	X		X			X		X	X	X	
Breaks	X		X	X	X	X		X	X	X	
Closing	X	X	X	X		X		X		X	

INDEX

ABOUT THE AUTHOR

Lenn Millbower is an accomplished training and entertainment professional. He has performed extensively throughout the United States as a musician-magician, has created and directed successful entertainment productions in venues ranging from nightclubs to theaters, and has composed and conducted music for many events. He has taught grade school, high school, and college-level students, and speaks frequently at adult education functions, including the American Society for Training and Development's 1999 and 2000 conferences. He has also written and conducted highly successful training seminars for Florida-based themed entertainment companies. Currently, Millbower is president of Offbeat Training, Inc.; a liberal arts professor at Southern College; and a training course writer residing in Orlando, Florida.

Millbower received his bachelor's of music in Composition from Berklee College of Music, Boston, Massachusetts, and his master's of arts in Human Resource Development from Webster University, St. Louis, Missouri. He is a member of the American Society for Training and Development and the National Business Education Association.

Offbeat Training™

Want more information about music and training?
Curious about other *Offbeat Training*™ techniques?
Want to contact Lenn Millbower?

Visit us on line at
www.offbeattraining.com